PE...
SECU...
POCKET
BOOK

written & illustrated
by
Rupert Godesen
HASP Training Ltd.

HASP
TRAINING
Hostile
Environment
Specialists

Produced and published by
Military Pocket Books Ltd.
www.milpkbk.co.uk

Military

Contents

Contents

1 ~ Introduction

Welcome

Welcome to your Personal Security pocket book, a guide to keeping yourself safe both at home and whilst travelling safely overseas. The book is very much a distillation of all my experiences over the last 25 years and I hope that you find it easy and enjoyable to read, I have certainly enjoyed writing it.

My globetrotting travelling days are by and large drawing to a close now (although I am not in a chair with a blanket on my knees just yet) so it's down to you guys reading this to pick up the baton.

Techniques which worked one year are not so relevant the next, the world changes all the time, so if you have any revelations or come across things that you think should be included for the benefit of your fellow travellers then do get in touch.
Even if it's just to say *"Hi"* it's always nice to hear about people's adventures and ideas. My contact details are at the end of this introduction.

You can also find a version for your smart phone when you down load the Military Pocket books app from the App Store.

About the Author

The Personal Security Pocket Book is the brainchild of Rupert Godesen, Managing Director of HASP Training and is a distillation of his experiences and knowledge gained over the last 25 years. Rupert has spent a quarter of a century in uniform serving throughout the world. When at home he trained the BBC staff both in the UK and abroad running Hostile environment courses for 6 years before setting up HASP Training.

There's a World Out There to Explore

The world we live in is a messy, noisy, wonderful hotchpotch mix of languages, cultures, terrains, climates, ideas and faiths. For which we should be truly grateful, differences should be celebrated, it makes life more interesting and varied.

Wouldn't it be mind bendingly dull if we were **all** roughly the same? We would all watch the same films, consume the same music, media, food and books. However with differences come numerous opportunities to offend, some go out of their way to offend/be offended due to resentments, jealousies, fear of their own shortcomings, in ignorance they lash out at the object of their frustration, the foreigner in their midst taking their jobs.

The jury's out as to whether the world is actually getting more dangerous or not, I don't think anyone can honestly say. But what is undeniable is that there's no longer any excuse for not knowing. In this internet age, if you can book a table for dinner, order a book, pizza or cinema tickets on your phone then you can jolly well find out the situation where you're travelling to.

Is the world getting more dangerous, or has it always been dangerous? Are we living in a permanent state of fear induced by a Government and a Press that love to emphasise the negative stories (to justify vast investment in Security services, Defence and other pet projects) or to flog papers. There are plenty of precautions that you can take to ensure you stay safe, which we'll cover in these pages.

Who's the Book for?

Hostile environment training has been around for the last twenty years and historically was aimed at journalists, but more and more "Duty of Care" is popping up on Human Resources managers radar as a **must have** prior to sending teams overseas to work.

Here are a few of the clients that Rupert has trained over the past few months while writing the book. A pair of very cheerful Oil and Gas men from Aberdeen working in Nigeria, a journalist from the Press Association covering the Christmas celebration in Kabul, a transport expert gathering information on the road networks in Northern Nigeria for service stations and truck stops.

An organisation helping to set up a tech hub in Libya to develop that forlorn country. A young doctor hoping to volunteer for MSF who wanted his eyes opened to the threats he might face, a concerned Mum travelling with her daughter for a few months. Two freelancers travelling to Syria to cover the war.

So you can see it's a fairly diverse group, but they had two things in common, firstly a desire to be prepared (organisations have a definite "Duty of Care" to their staff) and secondly they liked the "Prepare Not Scare" approach that HASP takes. Hostile environment training doesn't need to be hostile, there are lots of steps you can take to avoid the danger.

"Duty of care": It's become a bit of a buzz word nowadays and companies are discovering that it's considerably cheaper to pay for their staff to attend a HASP course than to have awkward questions asked in a court of law and then face a massive out of court settlement if/when an employee is harmed or killed whilst working abroad. When they have the book thrown at them.

An Unexpected Bonus

Few companies consider the fact, that by investing in these type of courses they are producing well informed, well prepared, confident members of staff that can operate safely whilst abroad, can carry out regular reviews and assessments of their own security and they in turn reflect well on their company.

What is HET?

Hostile Environment Training first came on the scene 20 or so years ago when the BBC turned to a few soldiers to run some form of preparation training for their journalists overseas. The BBC correctly foresaw that the days of the British "have a go hero", dressed as Alan Wicker were numbered. Just packing off your hack to God knows where with a waxed jacket, clean socks, a vague notion of the Empire's innate superiority and a British Passport as protection were not really sufficient anymore.

How the Book Works

Split into chapters that reflect what we teach on the course, the book follows a dialogue from your initial research at home before you go, through to arrival at your port of entry. Selecting a safe room in your hotel to dealing with a kidnap situation. If you're in a real hurry or want to remind yourself of the key points (as part of your weekly/daily review) then turn to the last page of each chapter where we've summarised.

To add a bit of colour and life, the book refers to numerous real life situations that have either happened to me personally or friends of mine.

In Useful links and research tools I have listed some of the superb sites, printed magazines and resources that I refer to regularly during my work and in putting this pocket book together.

Feedback to Us: The world changes constantly and we're keen to keep our skills and knowledge current so please email us to say what you thought worked where and what you think didn't, or just to say *"Hi"* and of course if you would like to attend one of our courses, or to pop down and pay a visit to see if it would fit your company's needs.

Rupert can be contacted at *rupert@hasptraining.co.uk* or visit the site *www.hasptraining.co.uk*

2 ~ I Just Need Some Travel Tips

Of course not all of you are going to be jetting off to work in South Sudan immunising children for 6 months, or travelling to Nigeria to arrange business deals. You might just want some travel advice. So the rest of this chapter will give you a few tips and things to think about when you're off on your hols. In the next chapter we'll look in more detail at why you're at risk.

Whilst travelling abroad it always pays to keep your wits about you, you're on your hols and it's time to chill out, do some sightseeing, ice cream and a few beers, but you're most likely in an unfamiliar place, with different customs, language, currency. You're on someone else's patch.

You shouldn't read this and think that everyone you meet beyond our borders is sizing you up to relieve you of your wallet and mug you, if we thought that then we wouldn't go anywhere. But you should still apply the 7 P's of Prior Preparation and Planning Prevents Pretty Poor Performance and always think "what if.... what if" this way nothing will come along and bite you in the rear.

PRIOR
PREPARATION
PLANNING
PREVENTS
PRETTY
POOR
PERFORMANCE

Disclosure of Information

When applying for or passing details to a third party we take little or total disregard for the information that we are handing over. The information that we give can appear harmless, however by giving an individual your name and date of birth will allow them to apply for credit cards or even to purchase items without you knowing. Simply by asking more about why the information is required or to whom the information is passed can prevent this from happening.

Social networking sites are a great way of communication with friends and family especially if you're working in another country. These sites can however harbour individuals that import **TROJANS** and software into the forums that can extract personal information from your computer or more importantly simply by adding an individual to a forum they can extract information from you regarding your personal life and details.

Certain sites are used frequently by journalists to extract an individual's information especially about their way of life or thoughts. These comments may appear innocent, however can be manipulated to be subversive to your organisation.

Electronic Security

The use of mobile phones, tablets and laptop computers form part of everyday life, we have been seduced by their cool functionality and use. However we pay very little attention to their security especially if the item becomes stolen or lost.

Simply locking these items with a pass lock can deter a would be thief or make it difficult for them to access these devices. Have you got some form of back up for all the data and information on your phone? If your bag was snatched tomorrow what would you lose, are all your passwords discretely stored? Thieves are technically proficient and are good at what they do. Stay one step ahead of them.

All laptops or PDA's should have anti-virus software and spy ware fitted to prevent your device being compromised and all your data lost, spy

ware can inform you if your device is being accessed by a third party, this is essential if bank details and personal information are stored on the device.

Leave/Holiday

We all deserve and enjoy a break, however it is at this time that our guard is down and we become more relaxed. Taking a holiday to a foreign country can be more relaxing than staying at home but can also produce problems if we let our security lapse. A passport can provide countries and individuals with a lot of information about your identity.

When travelling abroad you must ensure that your passport is secure and accounted for at all times, hiding it under the hotel mattress will not guarantee its safety. Most hotels have secure safes, but it should be noted that the hotel will have a spare key or that duplicate keys may have been produced. If your passport becomes lost

or stolen it should be reported immediately to the tour operator and if necessary to the local embassy who may assist in getting a temporary one issued.

Depending on which country you visit determines how vigilant you need to be of your surrounding and individuals. Do not set patterns when on holiday especially if a chosen route is dimly lit back to your hotel.

Stay in the well-lit areas and take the route that may be ten minutes longer and do not accept lifts from vehicles that are not registered taxis or appear genuine.

Get a couple of photocopies of your passport for an emergency, and keep them tucked away, make a note of the passport number, so at the very least you know that. Some journalists also take a digital scan of their passports and keep them on their memory sticks, and email them to themselves. Belt and braces.

Journalists are more likely to lose their passports from robbery and dodgy checkpoints than you are as a tourist, as they will be moving through conflict and contested areas often in their daily work, so need to have all the options covered when they have to prove their identities.

However be under no illusions, the team at the British Embassy or Consulate will not be thrilled to see you when you rock up with nothing but the shirt on your back, it's not like in the movies. They won't welcome you with open arms, they will probably keep you waiting for quite some time, it won't be fun, and you're trip will be trashed. If you stink of booze you're going to the bottom of the pile. However if you can demonstrate that you've prepared for this eventuality, have just been unlucky, and you can prove quickly who you are then you'll have an easier time.

Vehicle Security

Think about where you are going to park your vehicle when away from home, even if it is a short trip to town. Is the area well lit? If daytime have a look around the area and get a feel for lighting.

Are there other cars in the immediate vicinity, you may think you are saving yourself a couple of bob by parking somewhere off the beaten track but are you leaving yourself more vulnerable to vehicle crime? Again look at the state of the houses in the immediate vicinity, are they run down, does the area look dilapidated?

Sanitise the vehicle, remove all valuables, including your sat nav (thieves know to check the glove box!) and yes they will know you have one by the suction mark left on your windscreen. Do not leave bags anywhere on view even if empty. It will only serve as temptation to a potential thief. If you have to leave personal belongings in the vehicle then put them in the boot, try to remember to do it before leaving or if you must do it on arrival then drop the rear seats put the items in the boot, this means you don't broadcast then fact that you are putting stuff in your boot to anybody watching.

Large secured car parks probably offer the best protection for your vehicle although the good ones cost more it is probably advisable to use one when parking in cities. The last things you want is to be hit with a ticket for parking illegally or even worse towed away.

Internet/Social Networking

Used daily by most people conducting anything from research to online banking, it goes without saying that you should think about the information your put onto the World Wide Web because once it is on there it is there forever.

If using online banking then ensure you have an up to date and active anti-virus software protecting your computer. Some banks offer free system security downloads to protect your online accounts, but often will only cover your losses should you have made use of the free download so make sure you check the small print!

Social Networking

Facebook/Twitter/Bebo/Uniform Dating to name but a few, the internet has totally redesigned how we socialize and meet new people. The amount of personal information on social networking sites is astronomical. Below are a few things to bear in mind when putting personal information onto the internet:

Security – Is the website secure? Does the website display the padlock symbol at the bottom of the browser or does the web address start HTTPS when it asks for your information? Either of these should mean that you're connecting to a secure server. Only use sites which are secure so you can give yourself the best chance of protecting your data.

Passwords – Don't use the same password for all your accounts and make sure your password is complex not just your date of birth for example! Ensure your email account has a **good password** as this is where most of your password reminders will be sent.

Security Settings – Sites often have a habit of changing or introducing new features to "enhance" your online experience however you must be alert to possible changes in your security settings. Think about who can view your information, ideally family and friends only. Be alert to how the website uses your information, so when creating your online account, don't accept the default security setting, make sure you set it up to your expectation.

Do you really need to put the information on the internet to begin with? Think about what else is in photographs? Think about your backdrop, there could be stuff going on behind you that is not meant for others.

REMEMBER ONCE THE INFORMATION IS ON THE INTERNET IT IS ON THERE FOREVER, YOU CAN'T TAKE IT OFF.

Travel Security

UK Travel

Domestically the UK is a relatively secure environment in which to travel but large urban environments can quickly change into a potentially hostile area if only going for a night out in a city. Here are a few tips for UK travel:

Money – There are thousands of cash machines spread across the UK so there is no need to carry large sums of money around with you, if you don't have it you can't lose is or have it taken from you.

Nights out – If out with you mates, then stay with you mates! You are less likely to run into to trouble if you stay together.

Taxis – Beware of illegal taxis which operate predominately in large urban areas. Always use a company you know or pre book with a local firm, particularly if you are female.

Foreign Travel

Whether it be sunshine or adventure, people spend a great deal of time preparing for a foreign holiday, there are a few things you can do to ensure that you are correctly prepared to meet the challenges of the environment you will be in.

Pre-Holiday

Insurance – Make sure you get holiday insurance and ensure that it is fit for purpose, you will need a different level of cover for a skiing holiday than you would for a package holiday to Spain. Always check the small print! Falling foul of this will cost you a massive amount of £££ so if you're not sure if your policy covers you for the area you're going to better to find out when you can do something about it at home rather than facing a massive bill that you have no way of paying. Again the Embassy will not be too chuffed.

Security – If you are off the beaten track then make sure you carry out sufficient research on the country you intend to visit. There is a whole host of information on the internet written by people exploring the world, but as a basic ensure you understand cultural differences and get a feel for the security picture of the areas you intend to visit. Have a look at Chapter 7 for some useful research tools or look at the page on the HASP website.

Immunisation – Once you have researched your country of choice you should know what jabs you need and how far in advance you need to get them or start a course of anti-malarial tablets for example and ensure you take enough to see you through your trip.

Holiday Money

Do Not Leave It Till The Last Minute and Change Your Money at The Airport.

Your holiday money can be exchanged well in advance so don't get a poor exchange rate at the airport.
Sites such as www.moneysavingexpert.com can be a one stop shop to finding the best deal in your area. Do you need to travel with large amounts of currency? Or could you use a pre-paid credit/debit card or even travellers cheques to reduce the risk uninsured loss?

There are a lot of options out there and it pays to research this area well in advance of travel.

Passport – Ensure your passport is in date for the duration of your trip and bear in mind some countries have certain sensitivities if you have travelled to certain countries before arriving there. It pays to find out before you fly.

During Travel

Personal Security – It should go without saying that you should plan ahead for excursions or even when you set off into the unknown. Remember don't become a statistic, stick to well-lit areas in cities and beware of a "friendly" locals who want to give you a lift etc.

If you go out as a group then come back as a group. If you're unsure of an area, then ask about, ask the staff in the hotel, and if you are going to get a taxi, order it from the hotel, and insist that it comes to the front and picks you up.

When you get your holiday money, divide it up out of sight, preferably at home when you're waiting for the taxi, do it in the toilet. Don't leave it til you're in the arrivals hall and just about to jump into a taxi with everyone watching you.

Don't carry large sums of holiday money around and if you must don't flaunt it, split it up about your person/kit and the group. Carry some in your pockets and the rest in a hidden money belt or in your shoe, so if the worse comes to the worse then hopefully you won't lose the lot.

At the airport – thieves target the airports for a good reason, they find gullible travellers in abundance who are unaware of what's going on around them, quick to trust a smiling face, keen to get to the hotel/destination.

Don't get snared in a situation that you can't get out of, when you arrive there's no rush, if you're not feeling comfortable then grab a seat have a coffee and get your bearings, we are animals that rely on our senses, so use them, by taking half an hour to let the atmosphere wash over you, you'll be amazed at how much you can attune, and you'll step out a little more confident.

Accommodation – Hopefully your accommodation will have a coded safe for you to store your valuables in, they are good, however remember that the safes will have an override so tourists who forget their code can be reunited with their valuables! Even so this is probably the best place for your passport and travellers cheques.

Actions on Mugged or Worse ...

If you have been unfortunate enough to wind up in a mugging scenario then ensure you are complicit to the mugger's requests. Your primary aim is for you and your party to leave the encounter in one piece and not on a stretcher! Hand over your money and valuables, do not argue or appear aggressive, you only have one life, try to hang on to it!

Remember there are many parts of the world where life is cheap! Credit cards and travellers cheques can be cancelled and refunded, passports reissued, new clothes, watches purchased, life cannot be refunded.

Lost/Stolen Passport

Your first contact is the British Embassy/Consulate, however it is not like the movies where you can sprint in and they will sit you down and give you dinner and a change of clothes and within the hour present you with a new passport! It can take days to rectify these situations, remember it pays to be prepared.

Having already taken a photocopy of your passport you can present that to the officials to help speed things along and show that you have at least thought about the eventuality. As a bare minimum ensure you have written down a copy of your passport number and issue and expiry dates.

Though thought provoking you're not going to find a solution to every type of situation here and every scene is different This chapter is not designed to put you off foreign travel but merely to remind you that taking the time to plan for eventualities means that you can have a good time without being caught out in the unlikely event that things go wrong! Remember to adventure is to live.

In Summary

- Hostile environment training makes for well rounded, prepared staff that are self-reliant and reflect well on your company
- Don't underestimate the risks, but don't overestimate them either
- The **7 Ps - P**rior planning and **p**reparation **p**revent **p**retty **p**oor **p**erformance
- Be vigilant and protect with your personal information
- Putting information on the internet means it's on there forever
- Don't have the same password for everything and avoid your DOB
- Look after your passport
- Make copies of all your important documents
- Ensure your travel insurance is fit for purpose
- Leave your car somewhere safe and don't leave anything in it
- Thieves and conmen cluster around airports/ports so take extra care

- Don't carry lots of cash, but if you have to carry money distribute it around your pockets and your luggage, have small amounts handy for tips and cabs
- Stick to well-lit areas
- Let people know where you're going and for how long
- Be inquisitive, ask questions, find things out

3 ~ Why are You at Risk? "Why me?"

Deciding to Take that Job!

A crystal ball would be great wouldn't it? But predicting the outbreak of conflict and unrest can be quite tricky. Diplomats, governments and intelligence services spend millions (possibly billions) of dollars annually trying to do just that, and fail to see them coming with alarming regularity.

By the time you read this there may well be a couple of new wars that weren't happening when we sent the finished book to the printers. Criminals will continue to commit crimes, dictators will dictate and the front lines of conflicts will move over the planet in a rhythm that makes sense to few.

"Reports are emerging, that fierce fighting has broken out, in an area previously believed to be uninhabited"

But trouble spots and wars don't just pop up out of nowhere, there are usually warning signs (previous activity) or fighting and violence that might be a permanent fixture in that part of the world.

For example Guinea-Bissau was recently identified by the political scientist Jay Ulfelder as the country most likely to experience a coup, thanks to its toxic blend of greedy senior military officers, corruption and instability.

But the best predictor of violence and war is having one in the next door country, unrest and violence get passed from country-country in West Africa like an office cold. Shattered Afghanistan bred Al Qaeda, which then went on to inspire similar franchises like Al-Shabab in Somalia and Boko Haram in Nigeria.

What Makes a Country a Bad Land?

It's not the fast flowing rivers or the impassable valleys (although these sometimes do harbour some of the world's most dangerous individuals - far from the arm of the law with numerous places to hide out). The problem is written in the pages of the history books and is a potent mix of -

- Colonial meddling
- Legacy of Empires
- Proxy conflicts (think of the Cold War with the Soviet and American Empires encouraging local, regional forces to fight each other to protect their interests)
- Corruption
- Big business
- Highly questionable foreign policy

All these factors have careered like a bull in a china shop through these areas long before you and I set foot there. Helping shape prejudices and attitudes on both sides, handing power to a privileged minority and leaving the poor with no supporting infrastructure or hope for their children and nothing to live for.

This desperately unfair status quo benefits a small very wealthy band of the ruling elite (all around the globe, we're not talking about just one country here) who couldn't give less of a toss about the poor.

The West sends a vast amount of money (both officially and unofficially, via government aid programmes and charitable organisations – a friend told me a few weeks ago that the Masonic Lodges in the UK had sent in the region of £50 Million to the Philippines to help their relief effort) to countries like Pakistan to help alleviate the plight of the poor whilst there ruling elite seem oblivious to their suffering.

I was in Islamabad teaching a group of correspondents not long after the terrible flooding, I got chatting to a few of them and the general consensus was that those in power genuinely don't care.

"Why Me?"

There are lots of reasons why you might be on the receiving end of a casual spiteful remark or insult, a rock thrown at you, an opportunist mugging or a determined, targeted assault intent on harm.

It would be impossible to list them all here because they depend on the circumstances of the perpetrator (their background and prejudices) coupled with where you are, what you're wearing and what you're doing to piss them off, every case is unique.

But we'll look at the main ones, some common mistakes and things that you can avoid when planning your trip. For starters let's look at what you look like to others when you're on their patch and why drawing attention to yourself is unwise in some places.

What do You Look Like?

You look out of place and clearly don't belong, you might look substantially different to everyone else. Where I live in Bournemouth it's easy to spot foreign students as they walk around. They wear the same clothes and even have the same skin tone as locals, but there's just that something about the way they are walking or talking that makes them instantly recognisable.

Maybe they stand out because they're a certain age and waiting for the bus instead of cycling or driving like other local guys their age. Whatever the reason people who live there are acutely tuned into their surroundings and you stick out. It'll take a huge effort on your part to properly blend in completely.

There's not much point in trying to disguise yourself totally, and even if you did go to such great lengths you'd only arouse suspicion. You may find yourself being followed and maybe even dragged in for questioning. It is far safer to dress modestly in clothes that are respectful of local norms that are unlikely to draw the eye.

In parts of the world such as Libya where ethnicity and tribe are extremely important, tribes and other groups can be easily identified by the way they wear their head scarves, the greetings they use, the way they signal to one another in traffic.

So spare a thought for your appearance, you might not register walking through Terminal 5 with your pink Samsonite suitcase but you may well stick out like a sore thumb when you get to the other end.

You've Got Stuff

We are immeasurably better off than billions of people around the world. Relatively we want for nothing, so when you're planning your moves on foot, in taxis and as a tourist keep your expensive possessions out of sight. Better still leave them at home, only take items with you that you're prepared to lose, leave your heirloom ear rings and watches behind at home.

Make sure you have a contingency plan for continuing with your task if you lose all your stuff (due to light fingers or your bags going to Los Angeles not Lagos). Losing a phone or laptop with all your contacts, documents and emails could be a disaster and take you days to retrieve and make you look and feel a little unprofessional.

A gentleman on one of my courses had his iPhone snatched from his ear. He was in the back seat of a Nairobi taxi on a roundabout traveling at about 20 miles/hour at 2 o'clock in the morning. A lad on a scooter drew up alongside him and that was the last he saw of it.

Luckily he had written all the numbers and addresses down that he needed for the next 48 hours and his firm sorted him out with another phone. But you can just imagine what a headache it would have been if he'd lost it and everything on it.

So when you're in your taxi it's doors locked and windows up, there's much more on this topic in Chapters 12 and 17.

You Look Like an Easy Target

There's a lot to be said for sounding and looking "confident", it says a lot about you, I have to make calls to companies selling my courses and I won't lie to you I absolutely hate it.

Nobody likes to be sold stuff over the phone, but I try to make myself sound confident and that gives the impression that I deserve their time and their business, if I was a bundle of nerves I wouldn't get far.

When the British Army's Parachute Regiment drove into Freetown in Sierra Leone to prevent a massacre by the advancing West Side Boys (WSB), the bad guys had their eyes on them from the minute they landed sizing them up.

If they'd looked like an ill-disciplined bunch of scruffs whose drills were a bit sloppy then WSB would have wasted little time in taking them on to make a bold statement that this was their town.

But the Paras sent a message of their own to WSB, they arrived looking prepared, ready and "up for it" their drills were slick they looked fit, tough and hard and ready to go the distance (have I got room for another cliché? no I guess not) so WSB did the sensible thing and kept away.

So don't make it easy for the thieves, conmen, beggars and pick pockets that throng around ports of entry, airports, bus stations and hotels. Have everything to hand when you need it, be that your passport, multiple passport photos for passes, small bills for tips and the taxi to a few local phrases, you might feel like a fish out of water but try and look like you own the place. We'll look at this in more detail later.

Grinding Poverty

It's difficult to imagine as you sit on your sofa at home reading this, or in the departure lounge waiting for your flight, what it must feel like to have absolutely no possessions at all. To have absolutely no control over what happens to you, no hope of achieving anything meaningful with your short, dreadfully tough life and no way of protecting or providing for your kids. But it's an uncomfortable fact (amongst a vast amount of similar statistics) that over half of the population in India don't even have a toilet.

In "Pirates Aboard" by Klaus Hympendahl, the author explains why fishermen are turning to piracy on the world's previously tranquil sea lanes and shore lines. At first he paints us a pleasant scene some years ago of a couple pulling into a cove. They are approached by a local guy in a dugout canoe who  fishes the cove and the surrounding waters, he's done it all his life.

The sailor and the fisherman exchange greetings (they can't understand one anothers language, but they are both men plying the waters on their separate quests and find a way of communicating) the sailor purchases some fish and gives the fisherman a t-shirt and some cigarettes. They converse, smoke, laugh and the following day he leaves with a cheerful wave and everyone's happy.

Meanwhile Back in The Real World

Yanking us from that idyllic scene back to the present day, and now that same tranquil bay is packed with boats, the sailors view the fishermen as threats because Yacht Monthly and the internet has listed plenty of robberies on-board. They probably throw fag buts over the side and empty their toilets in the bay too.

The suspicious visitors don't buy anything from the fishermen, there's no dialogue at all and the guys on the land are getting poorer and poorer as time passes. It's not long before they start to resent these arrogant unlooked for visitors who bring nothing, rumours spread of topless women and alcohol and soon they decide to pounce.

Move Along Now!!

The Government of Botswana forcibly removed several indigenous tribes from their ancestral lands "to bring them out of the stone age". But they were no doubt quite

happy back there and in any case the real reason was so that authorities could get their hands on the diamonds beneath the ground.

The tribes were now effectively caged and saw nothing of this wealth, they were housed in camps and eventually succumbed to alcohol and HIV, as well as falling prey to the crime that lurks in such places.

You don't need to have Masters Degrees or an MBA to realise that the board/shareholders are interested in profits, not poor people.

What You Represent

We all judge books by their covers and make value judgements in seconds when we see someone. We'll steer clear of someone in the park if they've got a nasty looking dog, "He's got that frightening, intimidating dog for a reason" and the same is true when we're overseas. The locals will look at you and make a quick judgement.

In much of the developing world Illiteracy is endemic, locals will use what they can see to form an opinion of you. If you're sporting a Nike logo on your t-shirt or a BBC logo or any other symbol you'll more than likely be saying to them "I buy into the corporate strategy of this company".

So wouldn't it be better to just look plain and boring? Alright you're not going to get an upgrade when you board your flight, but nobody's going to get cross with you for looking drab, inoffensive and just slipping past them unnoticed like another person in a cab or on the street.

If getting an upgrade is that important to you then carry your scruffy clothes in your hand luggage and change into them in your first class cabin while sipping the complimentary bubbles.

Learn a Little of the Local Customs

To arrive in someone else's country and show absolutely no interest in the language, culture, customs and to make a big show of not being prepared (ego and bravado at play here) and not to cover up when advised to is both foolish and disrespectful and will land you in hot water before long.

Life is often about compromise, you are getting something from the trip, maybe a couple of weeks of holiday or a business trip. It's not unreasonable that you should compromise and adhere to the local rules. Some regimes will turn a blind eye to drinking for example but do not be fooled. If you take advantage then they may well descend with frightening speed and make an example of you.

Insensitivity to Local Customs

We sometimes find the customs and habits of foreigners perplexing and often downright offensive, (my brother in law lives in China and for the first couple of months found the spitting a bit off putting) "How can they have that attitude to women or children even to animals in the 21st Century? And why should I have to pay a bribe to get through this checkpoint to my place of work, something should be done about it?"

But it's not your business to be judge and jury, during your stay in **THEIR COUNTRY** you must be an impartial, broad minded ambassador for your country and to demonstrate the benefits of your culture. You're there to achieve your business goal or attain your aim during your trip and to get safely home, having left nothing but footprints and taken nothing but photos. You are on someone else's patch and you should move through it cautiously, slowly and respectfully.

Don't be fearful of making small mistakes though, if you do it warmly and with a smile then the majority of people will appreciate your attempts and correct you. You're making an effort.

We've Got Nothing they Want

Apart from £££ and business opportunities and a chance to get access to some of the rewards, it may very well be the case that we've got nothing they want. The renowned historian Eric Hobsbawn put it like this -

> "We have nothing to teach these people, none of our lessons are applicable, free market snake oil won't work. Democracy won't necessarily work. Nothing we export is necessarily going to work. They are all going to have to find their own way".

Just because it works over here doesn't guarantee success elsewhere, the world is such a diverse place. I read an article in Monocle magazine (buy it at your newsagents it's superb) about a popular flat sharing scheme operating in Japan. In order to provide cheap, clean accommodation in the city for young entrepreneurs, a building was converted into a grown up dormitory to house up to 20 young people.

Each of the young professionals had their own small room but shared washing and cooking facilities as well as sharing a large common room with a library, table tennis table, TV that kind of thing. They also had shared responsibility for keeping the place tidy, emptying the bins etc...

The article lauded the scheme but at the end of it, correctly pointed out that it had little chance of working outside of Japan and certainly not in the UK. It would fall apart within a month. Why? Because it is a model built around the Japanese's unique sense of neighbourliness and cooperation, it's not just a building with a load of furniture and white goods in, it's a model that works because the Japanese youngsters make it work.

You're an Idiot

It's just possible that you (probably not because you've bought this fine book) or one of your team is in fact just a good old fashioned idiot. You can offer someone the best advice and precautions available and they still get themselves in trouble. The cause might be arrogance, an innate rejection of authority, denial of the risks (denial is a strategy, it's a bad one, but a strategy nonetheless) or maybe bravado. They might be the "old sweat" who feels that the danger is part of the job and won't listen to any advice.

Or a toxic mix of all of them. It's unlikely that the idiot in the team would have got this far in the book so I think you can rule yourself out, but watch out for signs of complacency in yourself and your team.

Keeping One Foot on the Ground

Preferably two. At the beginning of The Lord of the Rings trilogy (bear with me here), Bilbo Baggins has a bit of advice for Frodo as he sets off on his journey to Mordor. *"It's a dangerous business setting out on the road my lad, if you don't keep your feet there's no telling where you'll be swept off to"*.

In Brief

- Do some research into where you're going see our chapter useful links and research tools
- Think about what you might look like to the locals when you get there
- Dress unobtrusively, be sensitive to local norms
- Keep all your valuables out of sight and leave expensive items at home
- Don't let yourself down and be an easy target
- Be mindful of the grinding poverty all around you
- Learn some local customs and a few greetings
- Don't forget you're a guest in someone else's country
- You might not have anything they want
- Don't be a prat, listen to what people suggest

4 ~ Common Trends and Threats

In this chapter we'll look at a number threats to the traveller, vulnerable points for you to watch out for, as well as some of the careless practices that get people into trouble and lead them to part with their possessions on a non-voluntary basis.

I did some Parachuting with the Army when I was younger and more flexible than I am now. During my initial training I noticed a poster declaring that *"Knowledge Dispels Fear"*, the Instructors briefed us that we were undertaking a perfectly safe activity and before long we had faith in them, the kit

"Knowledge dispels fear"

we were using and the fear duly diminished significantly.

There's no way to protect yourself 100% even in the sanctuary of your own home, but being aware of what you might face will greatly increase your confidence.

Kidnapping

Kidnap of individuals for the purposes of securing a monetary reward or ransom, is known colloquially as K&R. When I pose the question during my courses *"What do you see as the primary threat to your safety?"* it's normally kidnapping that comes out on top.

Columbia, which was home to the murderous Cali and Medellin drug cartels used to be the Kidnap capital of the world. However after a concerted effort by both the Governments of Colombia and the US this sorry accolade has now passed to Mexico.

An ongoing peace initiative between Colombia's Government and the FARC guerrillas was followed by foreign investment and renewed confidence in the country. Drugs continue to be a problem for Colombia but it now no longer dominates everyday life there as it once did.

It's likely that the regeneration that happened to Colombia will happen to Mexico eventually and many forecasters think post drug problem-Mexico will be an economic force to rival even the US. But this is some way off yet and for now it is a dangerous place for travellers to certain areas.

Express Kidnapping

Some organised crime gangs count taxi and coach drivers in their ranks, coercing them to work for them under threat of violence or intimidation. A coach driver (operating on a route maybe from an airport or a business area where pickings might be good) under orders from the gang picks up a load of passengers. He drives them

to a town or an area which is not on the route, but controlled by the gang.

The driver then pretends that the vehicle has broken down, that he has driven over his safe hours, has to stop to help a relative, any number of excuses. Or just orders the passengers out. Whatever the reason the passengers are left stranded at the mercy of the gang members who cluster around them either robbing them directly or offering them cab rides but at hugely inflated prices – highway robbery.

Virtual Kidnapping

Members of the Spanish pop group Delorean became the latest victims of a phenomenon of "virtual kidnapping" when they played gigs in Mexico City. A man posing as a hotel security officer phoned them and warned them that for their own safety they should move hotels, which they duly did.

In their new hotel they were contacted by members of the Zetas Cartel and told that they were being watched and would be killed if they left their rooms. The cartel told them to contact their families and arrange for a £940, 000 ransom to be paid. 30 hours into their ordeal they were freed from their rooms but it's unclear if it was paid.

(Dr Syrita Robinson lectures at Lancaster University on Survival Psychology has written a detailed study of the subject of kidnapping for the Personal Security Pocket book, Chapter 17)

The Ever Changing Threat

You may have read in the papers that antibiotics are becoming less affective in treatment as bugs become resilient to them, they are constantly evolving and adapting. The same can be said of criminals and other elements that seek to prey on the naïve and unwary traveller. Crime is stamped out in one area as a result of a big drive/initiative with hundreds of troops and police on the streets, only to pop up in another.

In 2012 the Nigerian Government cleared a huge area in the north of the country of criminals and the Boko Haram (The extremist Islamist group) who were operating a reign of terror. It was initially hailed as a success, but all the bad guys did was jump in their cars and trucks and take it to the other side of the country where they resumed their nefarious activities.

It is sometimes said that violence in the West African states (indeed through much of Africa) gets passed around like an office cold, crossing borders and reigniting just when the local population and the International community were breathing a sigh of relief. At the time of writing South Sudan has descended once more into violence after a few years of prosperity and reconstruction.

Criminals are really very good at what they do, and some groups are often well disciplined and organised. Why? Because it's how they earn their living.

Pick Pocketing Gangs

A criminal group from Eastern Europe were operating a pickpocketing ring in London. Disciplined, determined and organised they worked hard and sent all their ill-gotten gains back east, building lavish villas and farms to support their families, while at the same time claiming benefits in the UK.

They knew the system and how to play it and didn't conform to our idea of criminals at all.

Pick pockets and gangs proliferate in crowded areas like railway and bus stations, in fact anywhere where humanity is jostling and bumping past one another where a shunt here and there won't raise an eyebrow. Keep your bags zipped up and on the front of your body if possible, don't keep your wallet or your phone in your  back pocket unless you want to lose them. Keep all zips done up and be vigilant, make it difficult for them, they're dextrous and subtle and prey on the unwary.

Female Gang in Brazil

We have a mental image of what a criminal gang should look like, swarthy, intimidating, aggressive and violent, definitely not a group of attractive young women that would turn heads. But just such a gang used this to their advantage in the expensive shopping malls of the Brazilian city of Rio.

The girls patrolled the malls looking for wealthy female shoppers on their own, follow them to their cars, engaging them in conversation. They would use threats of violence and appalling retribution on their families if they went to the authorities and then take them on a shopping spree often emptying their bank accounts at ATMs.

You can just imagine that a middle aged woman in a smart 4x4 in a mall car park, arguing heatedly with three pretty young girls would draw little more than a smirk from a passer-by who sees a Mum with three precocious daughters, they wouldn't have been thinking that she was being held up. They got away with it for a few weeks and stole tens of thousands of dollars before being apprehended.

Airports and Other Choke Points

Thieves and conmen congregate around entry points like airports, ports and coach/bus terminals for one reason, to catch the unwary, new in town, gullible and to persuade them to part with their possessions. Criminals don't look for a challenge each day like those cheeky likeable thieves in Oliver Twist, they go for the easy "score" so you need to try and make it as hard as possible for them to pinch your stuff and to rip you off.

Robbery and Mugging

Despite what you see in the movies when our hero takes on the mugger, kicks the stuffing out of him and walks away with his ego intact, this is pure fantasy. If you asked these actors what they would do if they were mugged in real life they would most likely all say *"I'd hand my wallet and watch over as quickly as possible and back away"*. Hopefully you won't be wearing an expensive watch, or carrying too much cash and it's all insured. In Ch. 13 we'll cover what to do to protect yourself when you're out and about.

Arrogance

"The locals love me, they'd warn me if I was at risk, now back off you're cramping my style", I heard this account from a friend of mine who was on the security team of a famous (for all the wrong reasons sadly) individual who came to a very sticky end. He was ignoring all their advice about his behaviour and the effect it was having.

You may very well be a hot shot back on your patch, but never forget that you are a guest in someone else's country and it's up to you if you're seen as a welcome guest or an unwelcome guest. Don't make it easy for them to resent, mistrust, despise or dislike you.

Denial

Where there is denial, *"It'll never happen to me"* there is usually something to deny. As we'll explore later in Dr Robinson's Chapter on Kidnap & Ransom, denial is not a useful tactic when embarking on a trip into an unsafe area. We don't want to confront the possibility that we might come to harm, denial is a psychologically protective strategy, and facing up to the danger will require action and expense.

However denial is still quite common, how often do you check your smoke alarm or C02 alarm in

> **"Denial is a strategy... But it's not a very good one"**

your home, do you even have on? I admit that as a young man it didn't really cross my mind, but now that I have a young family, it's something I take seriously.

Having the right attitude is important as well as having the right kit. As part of our courses we provide "grab bags" full of essential kit designed to save you £££ as well as time wandering around the shops.

There are a number of rather smug, aggravating phrases around such as *"Failure to prepare is to prepare to fail"* and *"The beauty of not preparing is that failure comes as a complete surprise and is not preceded by a long period of worry and anxiety"* which do in fact make a lot of sense.

Complacency

We all have occasions when we switch off for a while, you can't be 100% alert all the time, but you should endeavour to stay on top of it until you get somewhere safe and secure. You can then let your guard down knowing that someone's got your back.

Lapses in concentration are one thing, but complacency is something different. A friend of mine once told me how he'd come to London to work after 26 years living in the Colombian capital Bogota, at the time the kidnapping centre of the world. *"In all those years at home I had never been mugged, robbed or assaulted, let alone kidnapped, neither had any of my family. We stuck to the security rules and were always careful".*

> # "It will never happen to me"

But within just three weeks of arriving in London he had been badly beaten up and robbed by an illegal taxi driver who had picked him up, breaking his leg with a steel pipe, taking his camera, laptop and valuables. He had let his guard down and felt free to wander wherever he pleased.

When I first drove over a covered drain in Afghanistan (a vulnerable choke point that the Taliban used to place IEDs to catch patrols unawares) in my soft skinned WMIK Land Rover the experienced soldier next to me looked over at me and asked me how I felt driving over it. I had been very apprehensive and he said to me *"Never forget to listen to those feelings mate and you'll be ok"*.

Alcohol and Drugs

Alcohol and drug abuse leaves the tax payer in this country with a massive bill. The police keeping drunks from fighting one another, doormen keeping idiots out of pubs, nurses and doctors picking up the pieces and stitching them up and social services rehousing kids with foster families.

We'd all be much better off if everyone drank sensibly, at home and in moderation wouldn't we?

If you're reliant or addicted to anything be it drugs, booze or cigarettes you are at a disadvantage. Addiction is a form of psychological dependence, and casts a cloud of need over you.

Alcohol distorts your reality, makes you carefree and careless, overly trusting and blind to the consequences, until of course you wake up in the cold light of dawn. So if you're a party animal try and reign it in if you can when you're working or overseas and postpone the partying till you're on home turf and can really let your hair down.

In Yemen and the Horn of Africa a scourge exists in the form of a flowering bush called Khat, a tradition which goes back a thousand years which sees the population succumb to a lifelong habit of addiction, chewing the freshly picked leaves. Khat chewers will work for the morning and then soon after lunch they'll start chewing and head home to pass the rest of the day in a "God like haze" leaving the kids to do whatever they please which invariably means emulating their elders and chewing Khat.

In Summary

- The threat from kidnapping is very real and changing, moving from region to region as security improves/ deteriorates
- Do some research, don't assume or rely on out dated information
- Stay off the booze till you get home
- Express kidnapping occurs when coach drivers abandon their passengers to the mercy of criminal gangs
- Virtual kidnapping "Remain in your hotel room or we'll kill you"
- Pickpocketing gangs are sometimes well organised and don't conform to the stereotype of the street urchin
- Thieves and conmen cluster around airports and ports because there are easy pickings and a constant supply
- If you're mugged don't fight back, hand it over, your stuff's insured

- If you're not prepared to lose it, leave it at home
- Denial is a strategy, but I wouldn't recommend it
- Drinking distorts everything so do it at home or in a safe place

5 ~ Personal Security

Personal Security is not a dark art, it is common sense if you work every day in a job where security is important. During their careers they pick up a lot of tricks/tips and techniques from colleagues as well as from trial and error (some things work and others don't), it becomes second nature.

What I want to achieve with this book and on my courses is to distil these years of experience that have been undertaken by others into some easy to remember check lists for you to refer to that will come naturally over time with a little thought.

> **Personal Security is mostly common sense, but only once it has been pointed out to us**

Common sense and Intuition are gifts to be used, if the hairs on the back of your neck are on end then your subconscious has seen something, noticed a change in a normal pattern that your conscious hasn't spotted and is yelling at you to do something.

A friend of mine was in Libya not long ago with a team staying in a hotel frequented by Westerners. One day he started to feel anxious. He couldn't quite put his finger on it and tried to ignore it but it wouldn't go away. He asked around the hotel staff but nobody had any news, so he spent a few minutes looking at the street through the windows and then it came to him.

There were absolutely no taxis at the front of the hotel or passing in the street, none at all. It was normally thronging with them, he got the team to pack their gear and to be ready to move quickly. Within minutes the bureau fixers were arriving and taking them to the airport.

American Special Forces units had made an unsuccessful attempt to take someone out and a tide of anti-Western feeling was sweeping the city. The taxi drivers were staying away from their hotel because they knew it was popular with westerners and they were angry with them.

Your subconscious does a lot of your driving for you too, you can quite happily undertake a long drive and not really think about changing gear, steering and breaking you do it automatically without any conscious effort. So make sure you tune into it and listen to what it has to say.

In this chapter we'll look at the importance of:

1. Tuning in to Your New Environment or *"Switching on"*
2. Body Language how awareness of it can help you.
3. Clothing / Back packs / Footwear
4. Posture / Profile while filming - working
5. Hostile crowds

1. Tuning into Your New Environment

Soldiers refer to this as *"switching on"* or *"being switched on"* and it has entered normal speech nowadays, but what does it mean? I recently found a poster in an Army barracks and it read like this:

1. I am prepared
2. I will not be surprised
3. I am not a soft target
4. I am tired but I am still thinking
5. I am aware of my surroundings

Let's look at each in turn and imagine an everyday scenario. You have a meeting with a local elder/businessman in a village a 2 hour drive away from your offices. Taking you there will be a fixer/driver from your bureau called Hassan that you've not worked with before. Hassan has been recommended by another trusted driver though.

> **Fixers:** Many organisations use fixer/drivers to get things done in countries where they don't know the language or their way around, locally civilians who are well connected and can escort you around.

I Am Prepared

You've planned your day ahead, you know the timings (the new driver's picking you up from the hotel at 0935, name is Hassan, telephone: no +44 7844...... light blue minivan VRN (vehicle registration number) OE64 XFG). You're only planning to drive to the site of the meeting for a few hours and return late afternoon, but you've packed an overnight bag and informed your bureau that you might be overnighting.

Meetings do run over and you can never account for traffic and acts of God, landslides, hurricanes, storms etc.... You decide to hold a briefing the afternoon before you depart to go through the timings with the team and give Hassan a quick call to check he's ok with the 0935 start. You're prepared.

I Will Not be Surprised

Thinking ahead and planning will force you to run through the options and contingencies, like a mental rehearsal. *"If we get stuck overnight we'll need accommodation, food etc..."* *"Is anyone in the team on medication? If we have to overnight are they going to be ok?"* So that hopefully when you set off at 0935 you will be ready for things if/when they do go wrong, because they often do but you won't be surprised and what's more you'll have plans in place to deal with them.

I Am Not a Soft Target

Building on the two steps that we've taken so far, you decide to find out if there are any dodgy spots to avoid. You chat to an experienced colleague about your route to the village, asking her advice she mentions that there have been a few robberies and banditry along that stretch in the past few weeks.

However they took place in the early mornings on all occasions, you check this with the staff in the hotel over lunch in passing and Hassan agrees when you call him. You're not a soft target because you've done your homework and won't blindly blunder into trouble. Denial and Bravado, burying your head in the sand are bad strategies. Take some time to find out, be inquisitive or if you haven't got time then delegate.

I Am Tired but Still Thinking

"Tiredness Kills, Take a Break" a sign we see on the Motorways in the UK. The meeting has been long and intense and you're exhausted on the drive home, but try and stay awake and alert until you get back to the safety of your bureau or hotel, then you can switch off and get your head down (go to sleep).

Pay attention to your surroundings, if you nod off and are involved in a car crash and Hassan is badly hurt you might not have a clue where you are. He might have taken a short cut off the agreed/cleared route to save a bit of time. Any number of things might occur, so it's much better to keep your eyes open and stay alert until you're on safe ground. If there are a number of you in the car take it in turns.

I Am Aware of My Surroundings

When at home we quite often walk around with our minds elsewhere, thinking about work, money, relationships etc... We're familiar with our patch, walking home whilst texting, you even see people walking to work reading books.

The worst thing that could happen is we bump into someone or trip over and rip your trousers or your tights and lose a bit of dignity. But driving back from your meeting at the end of the day you need to be aware of your surroundings and keep an eye on what's going around you all the time.

2 - Body Language

When you're out and about, the way you position yourself when engaging with other people and your body language can influence perceptions and how situations develop. Mindful use of this can limit the speed at which conflict escalates and violence ensues.

You can tell a lot about what someone's thinking from what their body is doing, it's a reflection of what's going on inside their heads. I was in Bosnia in the mid-90s, a town called Bihac, our job that particular day was to go and have a chat with a hospital director about some issues that had come to the attention of the Brigade Commander (who was responsible for an area the size of Hampshire).

The Hospital director had been quite a hard man to get anything out of, I went along with the team that managed that sector to see why he was such a closed book. I was new in town and would be taking over from them so it was a meet and greet.

To my horror the guys that I was working with kept their sunglasses on throughout the entire meeting, despite all the training we had undergone. Talking through an interpreter they had their arms crossed, slouched in their chairs throughout and chatted to one another sharing "in jokes" in English and the odd giggle, while this fella sat there stony faced and uncooperative.

It made my skin crawl it was so embarrassing. Everything about their body language was saying to the Director *"I don't really give a s@@t about what you're saying or about you as a person"*. It was no surprise that the lads had got nothing out of him.

A few weeks later I went in to see him with a new guy on the team, as we climbed the stairs to his office I noticed that he had lots of amateur artwork on the walls.

I went in with no sunglasses on show, a big smile on my face, friendly handshake and introduced my new partner. We got chatting about the artwork up the stairs and it turned out that he sponsored local art fair each year to encourage local kids and talented individuals to paint and exhibit, he would then hang each year's winner in the hospital for all to see.

What was coming out of my mouth was congruent with what my body was doing, I was making lots of eye contact, smiling, leaning forward, relaxed and talking to him not to my interpreter. (For details on how to get the best from your interpreter have a look at Chapter 9) And there were no sunglasses in sight. What's more within an hour he starter speaking to us in English, he had understood everything the previous team had said, he just chose not to reveal it to them.

The Body Rarely Lies

People find it quite hard to lie with their bodies, go on have a go, try lying to someone you really don't like, it's quite hard. You'll find yourself fidgeting, you might blush, you might avoid making eye contact and our throats dry out. We are designed as creatures to communicate non verbally.

The most honest part of our bodies are our feet, they will betray a nervous, anxious person, also look for self-soothing like stroking a tie or toying with hair for instance. Skilled liars who routinely lie will probably be able to mask their true intentions but your average man on the street will exhibit telltale signals.

Positioning and body language can influence perceptions and how situations develop.
Mindful use of this can limit the speed at which conflict escalates and violence ensues.

We are designed to communicate with our body language, from the start of our lives as babies we recognize smiles and other gestures to find our way long before we understand words.

Most of the information that our brains absorb and use to make a judgment about the person we're talking to is done visually rather than from the words they say. You'd be surprised at how much, in a survey it was discovered that something like only 3% was down to what they were saying as opposed to how they looked and acted. Body language gives off clues that we can use to gauge how people are feeling and thinking and we can also use it to disguise our own feelings.

Involuntary Smiling and Laughing

In the K&R chapter you'll learn about your body's involuntary reactions to highly stressful situations, the "Fight or Flight" effect. With the immediate release of lots of adrenaline your body will want to do one of the other.

Occasionally what happens after this (should your body decide on neither "Fight" nor "Flight") is cognitive paralysis or freezing where you are literally rooted to the spot. Your brain can't process quickly enough what's happening to you.

I have seen several people do this in scenarios, driving round a corner we are confronted by armed vigilantes who have blocked the road with one of their vehicles.

They have weapons and look pretty unpleasant. The commander of the gang bangs angrily on the window and orders the delegate in the front seat next to me to lower the window, which he duly does.

The poor guy is so nervous from this point on that he can't speak, respond to questions or obey simple commands, his face is literally frozen into a smirk. The gang tough guy meanwhile thinks he's taking the piss out of him and starts to get extremely angry, which makes matters worse. His brain had frozen and it was all too much for him, I called a halt to the exercise for a minute, had a chat with him and reassured him that it was all ok.

He wanted to continue with the scenario and was ok from that moment on, but it was a valuable experience for him to have in a safe controlled environment. I think that the great benefit of undergoing this type of residential course is the inoculation that it provides. In a Medical setting a minute amount of the disease is introduced into the body to allow that body to produce antibodies to combat future infection.

By introducing people to stressful scenarios that they are unlikely to have ever experienced before, they can start the process (which is a highly personal one to each individual) of preparing to deal with it. I have little doubt that that delegate would have handled himself fine if he had come across something similar.

3 - Clothing Backpacks and Footwear

Clothing

Sensible clothing for the environment you're going to work in is a must, both to provide protection from the elements (sun/rain) but also from unfriendly eyes. Leave all your smart clothes at home and dress modestly and conservatively.

You won't win any fashion prizes but on the flip side very few people are going to get a bee in their bonnet, no one's going to get upset if you look drab, boring and inoffensive. Long sleeve tops and head coverings and long trousers for men and ladies. If things get nasty and you get involved in a riot situation or a large altercation then what you are wearing can have an impact too.

Hoodies can be grabbed from behind and used to drag you to the floor, and so can pony tails. Some people wear ID discs or passes round their necks, if they get grabbed it'll put you off balance you and you might go down. Tuck it inside your shirt or get one of the ones that breaks when yanked, because if hair, hoodie or ID holder is pulled it'll put you completely off balance and you'll be suddenly on the ground.

When you're on the ground with a rowdy mob moving about you it's almost impossible to get up again. If you start getting jostled and thumped and you're in the midst of a crowd then link arms if you can

Backpacks

If you get into a punch up/riot situation, angry hands and fists may be coming your way thick and fast. Anything

you have on you will doubtless be taken from you, just let it go. Your priority is to get out of there with all your colleagues safe and unhurt, your cameras and kit can be sacrificed. I'm not suggesting that at the first shaking fist you drop everything and leg it, but don't get into a scuffle and delay your get away over something that's insured.

If your backpack is on both shoulders then one hard tug from behind and you'll be on your back, wear your backpack on one shoulder so that you can easily let it slip if need be. Bicycle courier type bags can

be worn on the back and the front of the body, which means you can easily slip it across your front which is also ideal for keeping it in site and away from thieving little fingers too.

Footwear

Sturdy lace up footwear with ankle support like walking boots are recommended, I have seen plenty of photographs of the aftermath of riots and disasters, what they have in common are the shoes everywhere.

When people start running the first thing to come off are shoes, hundreds of people running and nobody looking where they're going heels get hit by toes and the shoes start to come off by the dozen. And as if by magic from out of nowhere will come the broken glass, sharp debris on the ground. Don't become a casualty yourself

4 - Posture/Profile While Working

What you look like and the posture that you and your team adopt, can have an impact on how you're seen and treated. Let's imagine that you're a research team conducting a survey in a suburb, you arrive with your teams, take charge and start working. You send them off to cover as much of the area as possible, you might do a bit of filming too. Time flies, you're all getting stuff done and an hour later an interested crowd has grown around you.

You ignore them and then things start to get a bit rowdy, you get jostled, parted, groped, (the commotion is attracting others now) one of your team Sam loses his temper and swears at someone and it all kicks off. You eventually extract yourself from the mob but Sam is missing, you last saw him go down amidst a flurry of fists. Scared, running now and being followed by the angry crowd you try and head back to the car, there's still no sign of Sam and god knows where the others are.

You can't quite remember where the car is, because during the last hour you've wandered around a bit and are disorientated but by some miracle you get back to the vehicle but Hassan is nowhere to be seen and the car's locked. You remember now that you said you'd be at least four hours, so he's probably gone to see his cousin who lives in one of the flats….. It's a very tight spot you're in and the crowd are closing in again.

STOP….. AND relax… Let's wind the clock back 90 minutes and do it again but this time we'll tweak it a bit. But before we do just a quick note on swearing, **JUST DON'T DO IT** not even in jest under your breath. Like your expensive watch, your weekend binge drinking habit leave it at home and get out of the habit of swearing. It can only cause offence.

I heard of an Italian climber on his way up Everest who tripped up over a stray rope that a Nepalese Sherpa had laid, a bit tired and obviously a bit of a plonker he called him a "Stupid Motherf@@@r" not realising that it would be taken literally which it wouldn't be if he'd been on a climbing wall in Milan. He was very nearly lynched. So just don't swear. If you have got a filthy mouth then why not try consciously giving it up for a month before you go.

5 - Hostile Crowds

Try Not to Get Caught up in the Crowd in the First Place

You and your team turn up in the suburb, and you settle into the café to get the feel of the place. You've already got Hassan to call ahead to an official who said he'd meet you in the café on the edge of the square and assist you. But rather annoyingly he hasn't shown up, so you get Hassan to ask a local official if it would be ok to conduct your work and he says that it should be fine as long as you don't photograph any of the women or girls.

Keep One member of the Group on Watch

Have you ever watched the Meerkats on BBC Wildlife, they always have one or two on watch standing on their hind legs while the others lounge around and eat. Geese do the same thing, the Roman Army used them as sentries on all four corners of their temporary camps and nobody could get near them without a honk of warning.

In mass casualty situations, Paramedics on the scene will nominate one of their number to take a step back from the blood and bandages, to keep an eye on the overall situation/atmosphere. Back in the square, nominate one of your team to be the Meerkat, he's not to operate equipment/ask questions as part of your survey he's there to keep an eye out. While the rest of the team are focussed in and concentrating on their work your Meerkat will be able to see and sense the mood changing around him.

Things might hot up, maybe a couple of likely lads pointing your way on mobiles, a vehicle with more young trouble makers turning up, some weapons arrive, trouble brewing, women and children leaving the area or being hustled away by their menfolk, these are all signs that it's time to finish up and hit the road.

Have an Agreed Duress Code word

Establish a duress code or a word which will alert the team that all is not well, a really useful technique is to imagine a set of traffic lights. If everything's fine you probably wouldn't need to keep repeating **"Green"** all the time but you can if only to stay in touch and keep everyone thinking about.

However if one of the team see or hear something that makes them feel uncomfortable then they should say **"Amber"**, and everyone should repeat it, sharpens up a bit, packs anything away that needs packing for a hasty exit. If **"Red"** is then called it's time to go now.

Maintain a Clear View/Route to the Vehicle

You tell Hassan that you're going to be about three hours or so, but he's to either stay with you or to wait in the car, as you may need to leave suddenly. Always try and either keep a clear line of sight to the vehicle or keep an eye on the roads you're walking down and make sure you know how to get back to it. Keeping an eye on the vehicle will ensure that you don't get blocked in.

Link Arms

If through no fault of your own you are surprised and the crowd turns nasty around you (they can develop really quickly sometimes), then try and stay calm, lower your cameras, and try and put them behind your backs out of sight. They may well be the cause of the aggravation, link arms, but try and have one hand free to move through the milieu and to protect your face and body.

Don't Fight Back

You're free arm is not for wind milling a path through the crowd, don't strike people, look what it did for John Prescott (Google – john Prescott punch), it didn't help

him and it won't help you. Don't fight or delay your escape by fighting over cameras and bags, it's all insured and can be replaced, you can't, so let it go.

I'm not suggesting that at the first jostle you jettison all your gear, use your common sense, you'll know

when a situation is beyond what you're capable of dealing with and going to get you badly hurt.

Don't GO DOWN

It's very hard indeed to get up when you're being set upon or have been pushed to the ground, if you are then try and curl up into a ball to protect yourself and wait it out or crawl away as soon as you can. It's much better to stay upright, if you have linked arms with a couple of the others and one of you takes a blow it's possible to still manoeuvre your way out of the throng.

Don't Leave Anyone Behind

No more need be said about this I don't think, you're not going to leave the square and drive back to the hotel without them are you? Of course not, so stay within arm's reach at all times and keep close, because if they do go down then you'll have to get them out of there somehow and that will be a nightmare.

Don't Run

A friend of mine was caught in a riot and every fibre in his being was screaming at him to "RRUUUUUUUUUUUUUUUN!" but he knew if he did that he'd be felled. Something strange happens to people in riots, they succumb to a temporary madness, a sort

of anything goes. If you run you're fair game and might get a brick, bottle or bullet. If you are able to keep your cool then walk calmly out of the trouble area, don't run with the crowd try and make your way at 90 degrees to them to a clearer area.

Thankfully you got your guys out ok on this occasion and made it back to the hotel with just a few cuts and bruises.

Hold a Regular Review

If you're the Team Leader why not implement weekly or regular meetings to review your procedures, keeping everyone in the loop, refresh and practice your procedures. Everyone should know where everyone else is staying, know the location/phone number of the nearest safe house/embassy. Know the Rendezvous and what to do in case on a handful of emergencies.

In summary

- Personal security is a series of common sense steps learned over time by trial and error
- *"Switch on"* - I am prepared, I won't be surprised, I am not a soft target, I am tired but thinking and aware of my surroundings
- Be aware of how the mindful use of body language can calm down or escalate the situation, because the body rarely lies
- Be careful of involuntary smiling and laughing
- When working in a group try and have one member of the team on watch
- Have a clear duress or warning code to let the others know that the lookout is nervous and wants to leave. When he makes the call listen to him, don't argue
- If you find yourself in a riot slip your backpack onto one shoulder, if it gets pulled you don't want to drop to the floor
- Don't run, instead try and make your way to one side
- Wear sturdy footwear
- Don't leave a colleague behind, it's better to stay close and in touch than to have to go back in
- Hold regular reviews of your security, even if it's just a couple of minutes each evening. It's a good habit to get into

6 ~ Pre-Trip Planning

Depending on who they work for, travellers will get varying amounts of time to prepare for an assignment, time spent in preparation will greatly increase your chances of success, and reduce the risk of complications and problems once in country.

The following three lists are things you should pay attention to when planning your trip, divided conveniently between **Research – Documentation – Equipment**

Research

1. The Political situation

2. In Country information sources and of course chapter 7 of this pocket book

3. Local religion, may affect what you wear

4. Attitude to foreigners, UK citizens, internationals and the press

5. Local laws (drinking etc…)

6. Curfews

7. Medical services

8. Hospitals/doctors/pharmacies/safe blood/needles

9. Local forces/law enforcement/army/militias

10. No go areas- dodgy parts of town

11. Use of local guides -recommended fixers

12. Previous experience - anyone in the organisation that's been there, lived there

13. Communications - how do you plan to communicate back to your office

14. Contacts - telephone/fax/email/sat phone/computer/ local infrastructure

15. Choice of airline -getting to and from

16. Logistic supplies - power/water/food/transport

17. Mapping

Documentation

1. Passport - if you can, get 2 passports

2. Visas - check no restrictions and the date of departure, don't get stuck there

3. ID photos for press passes (the more the merrier)

4. Documentation for all the equipment you're taking

5. Medical vaccinations (yellow card) make sure they are all in date, if you do a lot of travelling you'll need to keep them in date all the time

6. Medication - label it up in the proper containers

7. Currency - travellers cheques, credit cards, local currency, other useful currency, you may need two if you are crossing borders or one is not accepted in a certain area.

8. Insurance policy- evacuation plan.

9. Dictionary or phrase book, ice breakers

10. Risk assessment forms

11. Next of kin forms

12. Accommodation and car hire

13. Letters of accreditation

14. Addresses and contact list

15. Aids test certificate for some countries, in some countries if you haven't got one you'll get marched off to a centre and have to undergo one, or be refused entry.

16. License for satellite dish if appropriate

17. Will

Equipment

1. Work equipment

2. Torch and spare batteries

3. Penknife

4. Short wave radio

5. Wet wipes / loo paper

6. Universal sink plug

7. Gaffer tape

8. Bin bags

9. Travel adaptors

10. Sun glasses

11. Compass or GPS

12. Grab bag

13. Water purification

14. Water bottle
15. Water purification
16. Rape alarm
17. Pack safe
18. Door wedge
19. First aid kit
20. Sunscreen
21. Insect repellent
22. Malaria tabs
23. Ear plugs
24. Disinfectant

In the age of the internet none of us now have any excuse to turn up somewhere and not know the first things about customs and language or recent political activity. There are numerous resources on the web and a whole host of wonderful authors to delve into when you're doing some background reading.

Cast your net wide and read as much as you can, if you have plenty of notice prior to your trip why not dedicate 30 mins each day to researching it.

Reading Government websites will give you one perspective and it'll more than likely just list the bad things that are happening there (it's largely a back covering exercise "We told you not to go"), however if you also search the internet, talk to people, read books and accounts by intrepid travellers and authors who live their then you'll often get a different picture.

Pakistan for instance is the sort of place that you'd think you'll get lynched as soon as you get off the plane, but take time to read Anatol Lieven's book *Pakistan: A hard country* you'll discover that by taking precautions and moving carefully, much of the country can be explored relatively safely.

George RR Martin, author of Game of thrones once said *"A man who has read a thousand books has lived a thousand lives, but a man who has read only one has lived only one"*. The Army have a saying *"Time spent in recce is rarely wasted"* Eric Newby and his wife embarked on a 2000 mile dream trip from the foot of the Himalayas to the Indian Ocean navigating down the Ganges.

They set off in their beautiful rowing boat with a 40cm deep keel. The first 50 kilometres took them a week because they didn't know that the Ganges for most of its length is only 36cm deep. It made me chuckle when I read it but you can bet they weren't laughing when they discovered their problem.

Make sure you have a dental and medical check, especially if you've had problems with your teeth before. Book your flights well in advance and find out if you need visas and if you have to have specific entry requirements upon arrival, like an AIDS test certificate. My sister booked and paid for a flight to India only to discover 2 days before she was flying that she needed a visa and couldn't go on the holiday and lost her £££.

On luggage labels put an office address not your home address.

Always pack your bags yourself, that way you know what's in there and your friends haven't put a bb gun or something which seemed hilarious at the time but might land you in serious trouble, the same goes on the way home.

"Fail to prepare and you're preparing to fail"

Childlike Curiosity –

Don't stop asking questions when you arrive, just because you think you've done your homework, things can change rapidly, keep that inquisitive thing going on. Kids look, listen, and touch asking questions about everything that's how they suck up information so try a bit of that and you'll be more aware of what's around you.

7 ~ Useful Links and Research Tools

Books, magazines, specialist periodicals, clubs and websites are all good sources of information and inspiration, here are a few that I use regularly.

Buying Books – A Warning

Advice from one who's got the book buying bug. When you go into a book shop with an itchy credit card, just buy one book and read it/finish it and then go and buy the next one. Don't do what I used to do and buy three or four on a topic, start them all and finish none.

Half-finished books left open on table tops and arms of chairs are not good for the soul (bear with me) they are a metaphor for other unfinished things in your life, if you're going to start something then do so with the full intention of completing it.

If it's crap then donate it to the library and move onto the next one. But stick with it, you'll learn a **LOT MORE** reading one front to back than buying five and dipping into them. Not to mention having more ££££ in your pocket.

In this section I have listed a series of websites that I recommend to clients who attend my courses as sources of in country information. They are all excellent and some put on expos and discussions throughout the year. I have also included a handful of books that I have come across, some are country specific but are a fascinating read.

The Front Line Club

www.frontlineclub.com I was lucky enough to meet one of the founding members of the club at a conference and I try and attend talks and screenings whenever I can. Situated a stone's throw from Paddington railway station in London, check out the listings on their website for what's on. They also have an excellent series of podcasts that you can download.

Monocle Magazine

www.monocle.com Definitely my favourite magazine, they've got their own radio station too which you find on the App store, a beautiful magazine lovingly crafted featuring great photos, fashion, design, music and of course all important articles covering the important topics. Subscribers get access to their archive of stories and videos an indispensable tool for researching your trip and making a discovery.

The Week

A brilliant round up of the week's news (hence the name) if you don't have time to read the papers it's a great way to catch up on a Friday (that's when it arrives if you subscribe which is by far the cheapest option). **www.theweek.co.uk** Also check out the website which has a column entitled 10 things you need to know today.

The Economist

Don't be put off by the title, the magazine is not just about economics, it is an excellent weekly paper, which provides in depth analysis of current affairs around the globe.

Stanfords Map shop

In the heart of London's Covent Garden this is the most wonderful resource for travellers and lovely place to while away a few hours. **www.stanfords.co.uk**

Lonely Plant Guide Books

Without a doubt these are the books for up to date information that you can carry in your pocket, packed with phone numbers, prices, dining tips and lots more. If you're buying one on eBay make sure you don't get a 10 year old one as it might be out of date. **www.lonelyplanet.com**

Radio 4 Podcasts

Covering a huge range of topics, this is a superb resource, search the list for what you're after, download onto your phone and listen to them when you're on the road.

Waterstones Bookshop

With the most amazing travel section and usually a café on site, park yourself for an hour and familiarise yourself with every title and compare them.

The International Crisis Group

ICG is an organisation that has staff all over the world and compiles detailed, written reports and assessments that are used by Governments and NGOs, there in country experts regularly feature on the news and are widely consulted. Find them at **www.crisisgroup.org** and if you're feeling philanthropic why not donate some funds so that they can continue doing their excellent work that we all benefit from.

The Foreign and Commonwealth Office

The FCO website **www.gov.uk/foreign-travel-advice** is somewhat cautious in its outlook, preferring that its citizens refrain from going anywhere dangerous, but still a useful site.

Kidnap and Ransom Magazine

The editor Mark Lowe apart from being a thoroughly nice man is a hugely knowledgeable on the subject. Mark manages to make this subject highly accessible via his site, I refer to it regularly.

Find his work at **www.krmagazine.com**

Intersec

The Journal of International Security
www.intersecmag.co.uk

Mischa Glenny's book Macmafia

If you want an objective look at crime across the globe from Russia to Brazil then this is the one for you, I couldn't put it down.

Michael Ignattief series of Books

The Warrior's Honour, Blood and Belonging. Ignattief is a Canadian Academic who undertook a road trip to uncover why people are driven to kill and fight their neighbours, his journey uncovers some quite uncomfortable realities, he writes in an easy style.

Nothing to Envy

A book about North Korea which details the living conditions, it gives you an insight into what some regimes will do to remain in power and how they can brainwash their people.

Phone people up

Lots of people like to chat about their specialist subjects and feel flattered to be approached for advice, so don't be afraid of just picking the phone up and saying *"Hi there, look I am undertaking a trip to ... ... And I understand you've been there recently, could you spare me a few tip top tips, I'd really appreciate any help".* They can always say no.

The previous list contains links and books that I have personally come across, but if you've got any great reads or sites that you recommend, do let us know and we'll include them if they fit the bill.

8 ~ Living and Working in an Unfamiliar Environment

If you've been to boarding school you'll be familiar with the concept of "home sickness", but it might not be something you'd consider when you plan that long overseas assignment, it only effects kids right?

Long way from home - Obviously you're going to miss your wife and kids (boyfriend/girlfriend etc...) but if you're not mindful of it, the whole "differentness" of your situation might well get to you. Making you unhappy, withdrawn and ultimately less efficient and even a burden on your co-workers.

I have witnessed a couple of colleagues suffer from this kind of thing, they were quite different people from one another but shared one thing in common.

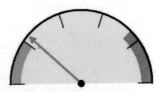

the "ha ha" needle

They didn't ask for or want any help, they pushed us away. One guy fell in love just before we flew (D'oh!!) and ended up running up a £2,000 mobile phone bill in 4 weeks which prompted Vodafone to call us in Bosnia. He just couldn't adjust to it and eventually was unable to do his job and had to be sent home.

The second guy (who sadly had been a good friend of mine) started talking in hushed tones to people half way through a tour of Afghanistan, which was annoying because we were all one big happy team. He began keeping secrets, gossiped and generally started to upset everybody, which in turn made them less likely to help him and he's still not right really to this day.

He started to go sick a lot, feigned a back injury, became withdrawn and aloof and wouldn't join in. It only really dawned on me later that ultimately we had failed him, we should have spotted what was happening and dealt with it, but we didn't we let him fall and I will always feel bad about it.

Working overseas, under pressure and in challenging places can also introduce you to unpleasant aspects of your own personality that your straight forward life and manageable stress levels at home might have masked.

That's why travel is sometimes referred to as a "Voyage of self-discovery", but you might not like what you find.

Travelling and working for long periods away from your patch can be a challenge in a number of different ways. It can be a stamina challenge, if you're putting in long unsociable hours relying on coffee, and not taking the time to eat properly, or take to time away from the coal face. It can also be an emotional challenge sometimes and occasionally a spiritual challenge. But it is rarely an intellectual challenge it's more a matter of common sense over intellect.

Living and working out of a suitcase is exhausting if you are not used to it. It has a strange unreality which is both unsettling and exciting at the same time. We are creatures of habit and routine, we like things a certain way, this might be a certain mug for our tea, have a certain routine in the morning.

I liken it to being outside all day long in the fresh air, at the end of the day you're completely worn out, you don't realise it but you've burnt a shed load more calories. And you collapse into bed.

Getting Ready

Try and get as much information about your working conditions and accommodation as you can, but be

prepared for a significant down grade in standards, this way disappointment won't come as a blow when you're rooms look nothing like the photos on the Internet or your working in a completely different compound and not with the team you thought you were with. Try and maintain a flexible, cheerful outlook.

Before you leave home take some time to visualise what it'll be like, you might be sharing a bedroom and a bathroom with others, it might be a walk down a few flights of stairs to get to the wash room, this way you can have a virtual tour of your surroundings, and make a list of what you will need, write it down as you think it.

You might need a pair of flip flops if the walk ways are dirty, so jot it all down and get it packed, but don't leave it till you get to the Airport to get it all in Boots because sods law dictates they won't have what you need or you'll get stuck in a tailback and have minutes to spare to make your flight.

Culture Shock

You may have heard of the phrase Culture Shock, but what does it actually mean? The Dictionary refers to it as:

> "A state of bewilderment and distress experienced by an individual who is suddenly exposed to a new, strange and foreign social and cultural environment"

Going Down – a Negative Experience

Someone having real difficulties will normally go through 5 distinct phases as things get progressively worse for them and they become unable to cope. Read each one in turn and think about what they mean to you.

1. **Strain** – you have to learn to converse in a new language, new currency and the associated psychological adaptations. Everything is different and confusing, rather than being new and exciting.
2. **Sense of loss** – friends, possessions and status.
3. **Rejection** – of your new culture and it of you.
4. **Confusion** – why do they treat their animals like that, what the hell is wrong with this bloody country? I hate it here.
5. **Impotence** – inability to cope with the new environment, you feel powerless and vulnerable.

Did they spark any thoughts in you? By being aware of the symptoms, you can begin to take steps to mitigate them in your own way, after all its true what they say and I apologise if I have written this in every chapter but "Knowledge is Power".

Going UP – a Positive Experience

More often than not you and your colleagues will have a positive experience, some people slot right in and thrive with a little bit of effort, but they'll still go through a number of phases when settling into a new culture:

1. The honeymoon
2. Crisis and disintegration
3. Reintegration
4. Autonomy
5. Independence

Drained and Depressed

If you're feeling a bit low then a drink with friends after work, some company and a giggle are a great way to lift you up out of your mood. But alcohol on its own and on your own is never the answer, drinking with friends to remember and reminisce is fine, but don't drink to make anything better, to cope or to forget. 9 times out of 10 drinking will have the opposite effect and compound the problem.

> ## "Drink to remember, not to forget"

It's important to relax, taking your mind off work and the pressures that you're under. Working yourself into the ground will ensure that your work suffers and you'll detract from the effectiveness of the team in the long run. Learn to look out for signs of exhaustion in your colleagues, acting out of character, alcohol dependency, grumpy, bad tempered etc....

Establish a Positive Routine

Get swiftly into a routine with your kit, washing, changing, shaving, resting, calling home, writing postcards etc... Many of us are creatures of routine, we sit at the same desks, we prefer a certain type of seat on a train, shave before getting in the shower, an unconscious comfort, a reassuring rhythm to life. Establishing a routine early on will really help you to settle in and it will reduce stress and anxiety.

Motivating Yourself, "Getting Stuff Done"

Be proactive

Begin with the end in mind

Put first things first

Think win-win

Seek first to understand and then to be understood

Synergise

Sharpen the saw.

In Summary

- Homesickness doesn't just affect kids, it can have a serious impact on adults too

- Do as much research and preparation into your new working conditions and job as you can

- Prepare mentally for a significant down grade in accommodation so when/if it happens you won't go into a flat spin

- Be aware of the debilitating effects of "Culture shock" – strain, sense of loss, rejection, confusion and impotence

- Make sure your glass is half full and no half empty

- If you are going to drink alcohol, do it to remember but not to cope, this never works

- Establish a positive routine as early as you can

9 ~ Using an Interpreter Effectively

English is spoken throughout the world, it is the language of business and music, luckily for us. But occasionally you'll need to either muddle through with sign language and your sense of humour, finding common themes.

If you talking seriously you may need use an Interpreter to communicate. Interpreting is a difficult art, here are a few tips on getting the most from your Interpreter or "Terp" and how control the situation.

They're Not a Piece of Software

There's a person under there too, so make an effort, you never know what tips and advice you may get from them as the day goes along.

Keep It Simple

Don't give them any information that is sensitive to your business or to the deal that they don't need to know. Assume that they are being debriefed at the end of the day by the Intelligence Services of their country, this is not an indicator that they are disloyal, it is just a fact of life in some parts of the world.

Consecutive or Simultaneous

Ask them if they will do consecutive or simultaneous interpreting, consecutive (one at a time) will give you lots more time to think about your responses and to watch the other guy for body language and other clues as to what he's thinking. Simultaneous however is a lot quicker and can save time and you can speak to more people, but it is exhausting for the terp and takes more practice to master.

You're doing the Talking

Make sure the terp doesn't start controlling the conversation and rabbiting away on his own excluding you, you're the one doing the talking not him and you're paying for his services.

Look your Subject in the Eye

When talking through your terp, don't look at him/her, look the person you're chatting to in the eye when you're talking to him, this will help to build rapport.

Make sure Your Terp is Comfortable

If they are nervous or intimidated by the conversation then have a duress signal that he can use to let you know.

Place Your Terp

Have the terp sit or stand by your side and slightly to the rear, he needs to be close enough to the subject to hear whispers and mumbles but not get between you and the subject.

Chit Chat

Always start the conversation with some light chit chat just to get things moving, everyone loves to chat and gossip, and it'll help build rapport. It's an important part of doing business in some cultures as well.

Keep it Nice and Slow

Give your terp time to interpret, break it into manageable chunks and use natural pauses.

Humour

Choose your jokes very carefully, some jokes don't translate well and it's easy to cause offence, another thing to bear in mind is the effect they may have on your terp. I was chatting to some gun toting villain in Bosnia in the 90s and I told him about an incident that happened to my Dad involving shotguns and whisky. I told the terp the first half which she passed on and then related the second half of the story. At this point my poor terp absolutely crumbled in hysterics, she laughed so much we had to abandon the interview.

Swearing and Cursing

Don't swear ever, at the very least it just makes you look ignorant and coarse, and at the worst it can cause serious offence, and when you have caused offence it's very hard to bring it back down and "uncause" it without some very skilful diplomacy. Assume they know what "fu@k" means most non English speaking people will recognise this word, so just don't use it.

Brief Your Terp

If you are going to be talking about something quite specific then let your terp know in advance so they can swot up on it, for example business French is quite different to ordering food and doing some sightseeing so give your terp the heads up if you can.

Properly Engage with Your Subject

Look them in the eye, not at your terp, just think of the terp as a mouthpiece and don't be embarrassed about ignoring them during the chat. If they are professional they will understand but if they're not then talk it through with them to put them at ease. Look attentive and smile even if you don't know exactly what they are saying, obviously not if they are telling you about a tragedy, use your inbuilt empathy.

Plan Your Time

Talking through an interpreter takes a more than half the time of a normal conversation so one of you needs to keep an eye on the clock, be mindful of local curfews and don't get caught out.

Try and Avoid Emotions

You will know if things are getting angry by the body language, remain calm, your terp may be able to calm things down by interpreting calmly and accurately and it's important that you stay calm too and that means keeping a lid on your body language.

Ensure Your Terp doesn't Answer

Make sure your terp just interprets your words, you don't want him answering questions regardless of how much he thinks he's helping, he can always ask you for clarification and can alert you if the subject hasn't understood.

They're Your Words

Ensure that the subject knows as well that the words are yours, not the terps and that the terp is just here to communicate, this might be important to protect the terp from angry reprisals when you're long gone.

Think about the Safety of Your Terp

Don't put your terp in a compromising position they still be there when you're gone, his or her family will not have the same level of protection that you do. If you are going to dangerous areas make sure your terp has access to body armour, medical kits and accommodation and water the same as the rest of the team. I have read of a few accounts where local terps and helpers have been left stranded while their wealthy western employers have been whisked to safety, which is completely unacceptable.

Don't Use Jargon

Jargon, slang and abbreviations don't help, your terp may not understand them and your subject definitely won't, so keep it simple.

Speak Direct

Don't say "ask him this" or "tell him that" just talk straight to your subject as if the terp wasn't there.

Treat your Terp Well

Give them some down time and let them relax, they do a hard job.

They Have Loyalty

Even if it's only to their salaries.

Speak Clearly

Don't let people shout over each other and recognise when it's time to call it a day.

10 ~ Arriving at Your Destination

JET LAG - This would seem an opportune moment to mention jet lag, with a little bit of thought and planning you can minimise its effects and be up and running quicker when you get there.

1. The rough idea is that it takes one day per hour of time difference to recover when travelling east and a bit less if you're heading west.

2. Some drugs like melatonin and modafinil can help combat jet lag, both are legal in the UK but you should always consult a doctor.

3. Try and adjust your sleep pattern before you depart, for example three days before you fly east force yourself to go to bed an hour earlier and get up an hour earlier and increase this by an hour a day until your departure. If you're going west do the reverse.

4. When you arrive you can help the adjustment by getting plenty of sun before midday which will stimulate your "wake up" hormones and then in the afternoon wear dark glasses and stay in the shade to stimulate your "go to bed" hormones.

5. Alcohol and caffeine will disturb sleep patterns so avoid them if possible.

In Chapter 6 we discussed areas that you could look at during your pre-trip planning including **Research – Documentation – Equipment**.

In this chapter we'll look at actually packing and getting yourself ready to walk out of the door and what to do when you get to your destination.

Valuables

Leave your valuable watch at home, if you aren't prepared to hand it over at a check point or barter it to get your camera or laptop back then take it off and get a cheap Casio from the garage. The same goes for your luggage, get yourself a scruffy looking grip or duffel bag so that it looks unremarkable on the baggage trolley.

Some airports have real problems with thieving by the ground crew from luggage, so try and make yours as inconspicuous as you can.

Money hidden

When you're packing your suitcase distribute your money about your suitcase and your person. Don't wait until you collect your hold luggage and are just about to walk out into Arrivals to get out your huge wedge of notes and start dishing them out to everyone. You're just asking for trouble.

Distribute your cash between your wallet, in books, money belt, shirt pockets and luggage. But I would also advise that you keep a note of where you've put it all. I lost $200 for a few days on honeymoon and it lead to quite an argument. Have a few small denomination bills ready in your trouser pocket to give to porters, taxi drivers etc...

Passport

Get a handful of colour photocopies of the identity page of your passport, laminate them so they look like ID cards and keep one handy in your pocket stowing the rest in your luggage. They're very useful if you get asked for ID by a stroppy official when outside a West African Airport, but remember don't try getting onto a plane with it.

A colleague of mine was getting into a taxi outside the Airport when a guard with a weapon tapped on the window and asked for his ID. Because he was still in the airport environment of course he handed over his passport, the guard then disappeared over a footbridge and into the night. He didn't follow him for obvious reasons and never saw it again.

Looking After your Documents

There will be plenty of documents relevant to your business and travel plans that you won't want to lose. Letters of accreditation, licenses to carry drugs, permits to film or to carry items of transmission or specific equipment etc...

If your day sack gets stolen and all your documents go with it, it could be a major drama and might delay the job for days if not longer.

Arrange for a colleague to carry spare copies separately, you can also scan them in and keep them all on a memory stick and wear that around your neck and if you wanted to take it a step further email them all to yourself. Cloud computing is a useful tool.

If you lose everything and turn up at the local Embassy with just the clothes on your back they will be much more willing to assist you and get you sorted out, if you can demonstrate that you took sensible precautions and were just unlucky.

Touch-Down You've Arrived

When you're strutting around H5 at Heathrow in your chinos and polo shirt, your Tag Heuer on your wrist, looking good (wondering how they're going to change the light bulbs in the roof) you'll probably pass by unnoticed by the other jet setters who are all thinking the same thing.

But have a thought for what you'll look like when you land. I'm not advocating that you dress like a vagrant and don't wash for ten days before you fly. But you can wear clothes that are a bit scruffy that will say "Nothing for you here fellas" to pickpockets and conmen at the other end.

If you're lucky enough to have come in on Business Class don't get off the aircraft first with the rest of the Execs. You'll immediately identify yourself as being worth robbing when you're the first through immigration. Wait until the rest of the passengers have got off and then join on the end. It'll give you a little more time to get your bearings and sort out that last minute bit of document admin or even time to change into your scruffs if you need to.

Immigration

Have all your documents to hand in a neat organised folder so you know where it all is. For example if you're carrying drugs or medicines you'll need paperwork for it. Having everything easily to hand will ensure that you don't accidentally flash any money around and get flustered.

You might be confronted by an aggressive, impatient looking official and there might be guns on show.

But you're just passing through with nothing to declare, you've no reason to look sheepish or guilty or to feel intimidated because you've not done anything wrong. A collection of passport style photos is really useful, they are easy to get hold of at railway stations and airports in the UK but can be a nightmare to get hold of when overseas, especially if you're in the airport and are close to getting through immigration.

Many countries insist that you register for this/that permit before you leave the terminal and you get pushed from one queue to the next. If you take 10 that should be plenty but certainly the BBC used to advise that the correspondents had 20 - 30 each, just in case.

A Few Dollars for Your Friends?

Low level bribery occurs frequently in places such as Nigeria, and if you dished a few dollars out every time someone asked you, you'd soon have an empty wallet. I took a cab to my hotel in Lagos from the airport and was asked for money about 10-12 times. It took the form of "You need a permit for this taxi" from a random bloke standing near the queue as I was jumping into the cab to "Something for your friends?" as I was getting the keys to my room.

If you haven't worked overseas before and are new to the whole experience you might think that you'd better just give them a few dollars because you don't want to make a scene.

But you wouldn't give someone a couple of quid in the newsagent at home would you? Or in the pub a girl approached you and asked for a bribe you'd look puzzled and say "No". You don't have to give anyone money in those circumstances. There are circumstances when it's sensible to give a small bribe or "donation" and we'll look at them in Chapter 14 Vehicle Check Points.

HIV/AIDS Certificate

Certain countries require an AIDS certificate demonstrating that you don't have the disease (some airports in Russia insist on this). I have read accounts of travellers arriving without the certificates that were marched to a clinic, made to submit to one and were then charged a fortune for it, so make sure you find out before you fly. Book early to avoid disappointment.

Being too prepared is much better than ill prepared, have contact numbers/addresses jotted down too. I had a holiday romance with a girl from Atlanta, Georgia and on the spur of the moment flew over to see her for a week.

It was only when I got to Immigration and was asked for the name and address of my host that I realised I didn't know her surname or address, we had been emailing one another and she was going to pick me up from the airport and I just knew her as Lizzie.

I wasn't allowed to turn on my phone to call her because we weren't in the arrivals hall yet, it took me about 40 minutes to convince the guy to let me through, and I was in the US with a British Army ID card, so not what you might consider a high risk individual.

Meeting a Fixer or Local Contact

You've got through immigration and are about to meet your fixer, you've spoken to him on the phone and confirmed that he's going to meet you.

I flew into Lagos and was due to be picked up by the company's fixer/driver called Valentine. He sounded like a decent guy, but when I emerged from Arrivals I saw this monster holding a clipboard with my name on it.

He must have been 7 feet tall, built like a tank complete with livid scar down one cheek, he would have looked far more at home on the set of "Game of Thrones" that waiting for me.

Surely the real Valentine had been hit on the head with a lead pipe and bundled into the boot of his car by this huge fella who had taken his placard and I was going to get a bit of the same.

So I ducked behind a pillar and called Valentines number and to my surprise he fished it out of his pocket and replied in a cheerful happy tone that I had heard in the UK "Hello Mr Rupert".

If it's your first time overseas you'll be a bit nervous about stepping out into the chaos awaiting outside with hawkers, salesmen, taxi drivers and everyone wanting a bit of you. Don't feel pressured into rushing head long into it, there's nothing wrong with taking a seat for 30 mins and getting your bearings.

If there are a few of you then collect your bags together and grab a corner and a coffee, or whatever they are serving up locally. Watching the ebb and flow of what's going on around you will settle you down and increase your confidence, you'll spot the officials, the permanent fixtures and the Information points. You can then approach them when you're ready.

If you're landing in a remote airfield and there are only a few flights a week, the locals scallywags will know when they're due in and will thin out when there's slim pickings, so waiting til the majority of the other passengers have gone it might quiet down a bit.

What if your fixer doesn't show? If he doesn't show your next course of action should be to call the bureau or office contact and arrange a pick up. If you're staying in a well-known hotel they might be willing to arrange a pick up for you.

Getting a cab. If you are feeling uneasy about getting a cab from the rank, ask the airport officials to arrange one for you. Don't follow the driver into a dark parking lot across the bridge and into the unknown where you'll be exposed.

Get the driver to bring the cab around to the front of the terminal. Agree the price before you get in, and ensure he knows where he's going, so if he gets lost then you're in a strong position to avoid getting ripped off. It will help to have the address of your destination written down on a piece of paper so you can show it to the driver.

Keep your eye on where you're going. I got a cab from Nairobi Airport to a game lodge north of the city to run some training for the BBC World Service. We agreed a price and the driver confirmed to me that he knew where he was going (although in hindsight the conversation consisted largely of me asking him questions and him replying "Yes Sir, yes Sir", which should have told me something.

I had done a map study on the internet, printed it out (though the scale was out) and I kept my eye on where he was going, so I knew we were on the right road at least. As it turned out he didn't know where it was at all, and we drove around for ages before I found it.

The Knowledge. London cabbies know the city like the backs of their hands, they don't get a licence until they have done the knowledge which proves they know the city well. But in many other countries taxi drivers know the city a bit and will rely on stopping regularly and asking locals as they home in on it. In my case my cabbie hadn't even heard of it before but all the lodges were on the same road.

He didn't want to lose the fare and hoped that I knew where it was and off we went. So don't assume that he knows where he's going. Stay Alert.

Actions in the Taxi

There is no hard and fast rule as to where to sit in the taxi, but one thing you should insist on is all Doors locked and windows up. I'm a bit of chatter box and in the UK I always like to sit in the front and chat to the driver. I wouldn't do it abroad though because other people can get into the back at lights or in traffic (if the locks don't work) and you don't want anyone sitting behind you that you can't see.

You don't need to talk to the taxi driver and some will remain silent throughout and drive. But sometimes taxi drivers work with criminal gangs and he might be sizing you and your luggage up to see if you're worth robbing.

They might ask you what you're doing, how long you'll be here, where you're from where you're planning to go during your stay. All information that they can use to arrange an unwelcome reception committee somewhere down the line.

Question, Questions ...

What's the best way to stop him asking you lots of question? Ask him lots of question. People love to talk and the majority of people love to talk about their favourite topic – themselves! Depending on where you are will depend on what's taboo, in Muslim countries it would be inappropriate to talk about your driver's wife and female children at length. Keeping him chatting will give you time to keep an eye on the road and also think of further questions to keep him going.

Stay off any controversial topics like Politics if you can as well as other topical things in the news that might get him upset, keep it light-hearted and good natured. Regardless of your background and upbringing most people have similar concerns, such as employment, children, the environment, old age etc… With a bit of imagination I am sure you can keep him talking for long enough.

Doors Locked and Windows Up

A friend of mine was in the back seat of a cab in Nairobi, driving around a roundabout at 20 mph, window open enjoying the warm night air and making a call on his iPhone. A young man swung alongside him and snatched it out of his hand. Even on the move there are still threats. In the major cities of some countries like South

> **"Doors locked Windows up"**

Africa, after dark nobody stops at red lights, they are haunted by gangs who will pounce if a car stops.

If you're travelling alone have your luggage next to you on the seats so you can keep your eye on it. Keep valuables out of sight, laptops bags and expensive looking flight cases in the foot wells. Where's the best place to sit? Sitting directly behind the driver he can't see you at all and psychologically it'll be easier for you to control/direct him. Sitting on the other side (the passenger side) you will still be behind him but you'll also have a clear view of what he's doing.

In Summary

- Jet lag can be managed, you can take steps to reduce its effects
- Leave valuables at home, expensive watches can be substituted with cheap ones
- Distribute your money throughout your pockets and luggage, but make a note of where it all is
- Take some colour copies of your passport, laminate them and keep one in your pocket in case you're asked for ID outside of the airport environment. But don't try and get on a plane with it
- You can back up all your important documents by photocopying them, emailing copies to yourself and keeping them all on a memory stick around your neck
- Dress down when you land so as not to draw attention
- Have a few passport photos in your wallet for unexpected passes and permits
- Find out what an acceptable small tip is, but ignore casual bribery
- You may have to get an HIV certificate to travel to some parts of the world
- Have a way of identifying your driver/fixer
- If you driver doesn't show, call the hotel/bureau and let them know, they may well dispatch another
- Make sure your driver knows where to go, but keep an eye out yourself as well
- Keep the doors locked and the windows up in the vehicle
- If you don't want the driver to ask you questions then ask him loads to keep him talking. But keep it light

11 ~ In your hotel

You've managed to get to the hotel, the first phase of your trip is nearly over but don't relax quite yet....

Get Dropped Right Outside

Don't get dropped off down the road and fobbed off with *"It's just down that track, you can't miss it"*, your cab driver might not have a clue where he is, and just wants to get paid and get shot of you.

Worse still he may be working with local criminals and routinely drops hapless travellers in their neighbourhood where they'll either fall prey to rogue cab drivers who will charge a small fortune or just rob you then and there.

Delay paying him until you're certain, insist he drives right up to the hotel and positively identify that it is in fact the correct hotel. If there are a few of you, jump out, pop in and confirm it.

Making your Entrance

Wouldn't it be great if all hotels employed trust worthy staff who are vetted and can be relied upon to look after both you and your possessions during your stay? The majority do, but I think it's safer to assume that you need to keep an eye on your possessions as much as is practical.

Some hotels like the larger more well-known ones, The Marriot in Islamabad and The Serena in Kabul, have robust external security that only allow access if you've got specific business or a booking. In these types of hotels you can relax a little bit more, they have an international reputation and are keen to maintain it.

Other hotels will allow access to anybody who cares to walk in and sit down, which means the hotel can't prevent people / undesirables / intelligence services from hanging around in the foyer and watching who is coming and going.

If you make a huge spectacle and behave like a teenage student ski trip yelling out one another's room numbers like a load of Hooray Henrys you're just making it easy for them to identify what rooms you're in. When they see you all in the bar later getting drunk, they might pop up into your room emptying your bags.

Don't Make a Scene

Don't behave like a Diva, apart from anything else if you make a big fuss the receptionists may decide to delay you even more just to screw you around a bit. I spent a week in one of those huge hotels in Moscow called the Seven Sisters.

When we arrived there were about 20 Brits and a handful of American businessmen, we were all tired and keen to check in to our rooms.

The first guy to get to the desk was from the US, unfortunately (for us all) he wasn't very polite, he was ill tempered and in a hurry, the Russian receptionist took an instant dislike to him and just shut the reception desk on him. She duly started doing her nails.

There must have been at least 15 desks stretching down this vast hall and just one desk where all the girls were just sitting chatting and winding this American up. He got more and more irate threatening to move his group to another hotel *"Fine"* they replied *"Go to another hotel that is your choice"*.

Seeing that this approach was not bearing fruit we sat on our bags, accepted that there was little we could do and occasionally smiled at the girls. Eventually they motioned us over and gave us our rooms. The Americans were still waiting when we came down to grab a cab into town half an hour later, none of us thought it was amusing as you can imagine.

Your Room Keys

When you have been issued your room keys put them straight in your pocket, don't leave them lying around for all to see, and the same goes in the restaurant, bar or the hotel café.

Nobody but you needs to know what hotel or room you're in. If you're part of a large group make a list of what rooms you're all in, if possible try and get rooms next to one another.

Many hotels will have safes (both in the rooms and in the reception) if they give you the code to the safe in your room, it means that a number of the hotel staff know it too.

The larger hotel safe in reception will have several people cleared to access it, so the only way you can be 100% certain of the security/safety of your items is keeping them on your person. Passports, documents, laptops and other items can all be kept at your feet in the bar, under the table in a restaurant.

Some hotels will demand that you relinquish your passport as part of the conditions of your stay in the hotel, I would protest at first, as nobody has the right to ask for your passport other than Government Officials, but in some countries you'll just have to.

Insist on a Safe Room?

If you're given a room that you're not happy with, don't be British about it and think *"Well I don't want to make a fuss"*. If you are given a dingy room at the back of the hotel, looking out onto a dark car park, with easy access to the street, on the ground floor, no bars on the windows, next to a fire escape which is propped open, march right back up to the reception and demand to be moved.

Ideally you'd want your entire party on the same floor or not too far from one another. I have threatened to move hotel before because they gave me a room like the one I just described and miraculously after a little shoulder shrugging and protest a room on the 1st or 2nd floor was found for me.

A 1st or 2nd floor room will require some planning and effort from a possible assailant to get in (which hopefully will put them off), but also it's not on the 7th floor so if you need to jump out of it and make a dash for the Embassy or your bureau because of attack, fire, whatever reason.

Ideally your room should be at the back of the hotel or one of the sides with clear route to get away from the hotel down a side street.

Time Spent in Recce... (Rarely Wasted)

Agree to meet back in the foyer in 10 mins and have a good look round the hotel. Familiarise yourself with the layout, entrance, exits and procedures you'll all adhere to and agree where to meet if something happens.

It's always advisable to go and actually visit the locations that you nominate, to avoid confusion. For example *"We'll meet at the front of the hotel"* does that mean the entrance where you came in or the restaurant/pool area that the staff refer to as the front?

The Army call these *"Actions On"* so for example if there's a fire alarm then the Actions On fire/alarm are meet at the fire assembly point. I recently trained a team to undertake some work in Libya, the security situation gradually deteriorated over a few days, until it was unsafe for them to be there.

They had an evacuation procedure which stipulated that upon receiving a call from the team leader they would grab their bags (which they kept permanently packed and by the door) make their way downstairs not using the lifts but the actual staircase, and meet in the rear part of the foyer away from view from the street, and head straight for the airport. They practised it a couple of times so when it happened they were able to get away quickly and with all their kit.

Review your Security Regularly

You can't think about security 24/7, you'd go potty and worry yourself unnecessarily. But it can't hurt each evening over dinner or at an allotted time to spend just 5 minutes reviewing the day and any security issues that arose. Discuss what happened and how you could improve on it. Security situations change as time goes by, threats escalate and diminish and you might chose to change your procedures to reflect this.

If you've just joined a team as the newbie don't be embarrassed about sticking your hand up and asking to be briefed on the procedures. The team might be old hands and all familiar with the drill and pay lip service to it. Don't slip into bad habits.

Securing your Possessions

Don't leave all your stuff lying in full view in your room, hotel staff can enter under the pretext that they were checking you are ok or cleaning. You are unlikely to turn someone into an opportunist murderer or rapist, but if you present them with an opportunity to steal something from you, with little chance of getting caught that is worth more than their annual wage they might lift it. So don't put temptation in their way.

Securing Yourself in your Room

There are a number of ways that you can secure yourself in your room to deter a casual intruder. On one occasion a hotel security guard on night shift walked into my room,

he'd tried the door to see if he could creep in and pinch something assuming I was in the bar.

If the door has a lock and security chain then these are your first line of defence, but some hotels locks are easily defeated. A door wedge jammed under the door will make it hard to gain access, make sure to fit in under the door handle and not the hinges. If it's placed under the hinges it'll be easily pushed open.

If there's a gap under the door place the wedge on a newspaper or magazine to give it some purchase. If you really want to scare him off (and wake up the whole hotel) a rape alarm taped either side of the door so when he barges in he gets an earful of digital screaming.

Furniture can be pushed against the door in an emergency and if you've opted for a twin you can place the unused bed against the door.

Dining

If you're eating in the hotel don't sit right out on the street with your keys on the table in full view of everyone walking past, your bags hung over the back of your chairs. If your keys and you are at the café then there's a good chance your rooms empty and worth a visit by a thief. The table at the front affords the sunniest spot with a great view of the bustling city street and the colourful locals passing by like an endless photo opportunity.

In countries where some elements of the population don't like Westerners and resent the relative luxury that you're afforded, it pays not to advertise/flaunt your presence. Stay inside the hotel at the back of the restaurant, out of sight from the street.

Getting Drunk

Alcohol is served discretely in some hotels, even in countries where they have strict rules banning it (I recently read about a brewery in Pakistan that exports beer to India, which was a bit of a surprise) mostly to encourage westerners to stay. Save your boozing for when you're at home would be my advice, plan a get together with the team and do it at home.

In a country where they don't like you to drink because it's against their beliefs, it's an easy thing to show a little restraint and respect.

In Summary

- Get dropped off AT your hotel, not a few streets away
- Don't make an unnecessary scene when you enter the hotel, but don't be fobbed off with unsuitable rooms either
- Make sure you know what rooms your colleagues are in
- Drop your bags in your rooms, then meet in the foyer for a safety brief and to identify where you'll meet if it all kicks off
- Don't leave expensive items lying around carelessly in your room it will only put temptation in someone's way
- Be clear on the emergency procedures
- Hold a regular security review/meeting
- Save the drinking till you're at home

12 ~ Out and About

Drinking

In Clint Eastwood's film Dirty Harry, he comes across a pervert lurking in the bushes while chasing a killer. The pervert cries *"If you're vice (the cops) I'll kill myself"* and Harry replies *"Well do it at home"*. I've heard so many stories about scrapes people have got into when they were pissed, my advice is just leave it until you get home. If you are going to drink then stay within your limits.

Your hosts or colleagues might egg you on, but keep your own mind and don't be pressured into doing anything. It's not big, it's not clever and it might land you in hot water.

A Sensitive Approach

If you make the odd cultural faux pas, don't head straight to the airport and flee the country. If you have taken a genuine interest in local customs and are visibly contrite when you get something wrong then you'll probably get away with it.

People are delighted when you can greet them in their own language and show interest in their way of life, but we can't be expected to know it all, all of the time.

So if you upset someone without meaning to, apologise profusely and genuinely, it's your first visit to their country, tell them where you're from and then ask them to advise you on what you did wrong.

And above all try and smile throughout, a smile has the most amazing power to win people over, but make sure you're genuinely apologetic and sincere. We are all experts in Body language without realising it (we've been doing it all our lives) and if you're insincere and taking the piss it will probably make matters worse.

Be Inquisitive

I have an advantage over most people because I am a chatterbox (although my wife might disagree sometimes) remember that a good source of knowledge is local people, taxi drivers, hotel staff, co-workers and locals. Try and ensure that you get your updates as to what's going on from as many sources as you can.

Let People Know Where you're Going

If you're going to go out separately from the rest of the team then make sure they know where you're going.

They have your number and vice versa, your phone has a full battery and tell them what time you're going to be back. Put yourself in their shoes, if you  said you were going to be back at 1100 and plans change and you're going on somewhere else then let them know so they're not flapping like hummingbirds, worrying about you.

They'll be very cross when you get back all cheerful to be met by a group of cross faces, and they may even have initiated emergency procedures which will take some explaining if you've cost the company money and made them look careless with safety.

You're Being Followed

Some countries and paranoid regimes will assign intelligence agencies to watch your every move, North Korea assigns minders that guide visitors to areas that they want you to see and away from things that they don't, such as the desperately poor areas.

China still escort foreigners around I believe, even in this day and age. Some covert operatives will be extremely professional and you'll never see them, others will be rubbish and you'll spot them a mile away.

Just accept that you're going to attract attention and may be routinely followed, but do not try and imitate Jason Bourne or 007 and attempt to give them the slip, even in jest. They won't find it amusing in the least and may even haul you in for questioning. *"Who taught you to undertake those counter surveillance techniques?"* "You work for MI6!!!" All the time you're regretting your silly prank. Another really good reason not to drink.

Bribes By Officials

Corruption is a fact of life and all that varies is the extent or the depth, from the scam centre of the world in Nigeria to the corridors of Westminster. Barely a day goes by without a story about someone caught with their hand in the till somewhere in the world. However as a rule of thumb the further away from the centre (capital city or centre of influence) you travel the more widespread and acceptable it becomes.

Corruption is a result of either 1. Individuals blatantly abusing their positions of authority for personal gain, or 2. Officials being so badly paid or not at all that they have to do it to survive and feed their families.

Bosnia in the mid-90s, I got chatting to a UN worker who was looking at border security to prevent drug trafficking and smuggling. He told me that border guards routinely accept bribes from drug traffickers to turn a blind eye.

> "These guards haven't been paid for months because their bosses cream the money off for themselves, leaving them with no money to feed their families. One day a charming, slick drug smuggler arrives at the check point, shares a fag with him, listens and empathises with his plight and then offers him a solution. He gives him the equivalent of a couple of months' salary to turn a blind to a few lorries that will be crossing at a certain time and there'll be more money coming his way in the future".

It's a no brainer really isn't it? You can let your family starve with a clean conscience or you can get on the gravy train like everyone else and secure some sort of a future for your family.

The wrong papers

A photographer friend of mine was detained by some officials on a trumped up charge of having the wrong permit to photograph. There was of course no such permit and they were demanding payment there and then.

So he stopped filming and firmly but respectfully said *"Well I'm not just giving you the money, let's go to the Police Station and I want a receipt"*. He didn't really have a choice at this point, if he had just told them to get lost then they would have arrested him to save face.

The best thing is to diffuse the situation and say "OK, I am sorry I didn't know I needed that, let's go and sort it out in your office". On this occasion they set off walking to the cop shop and half way there they changed their minds and left him to continue shooting.

Infuriating Bureaucracy

Sometimes however it won't end like the above example, you might literally be bounced from one office to another for days to get the right signatures, stamp, letters of reference without which you won't be able to carry out your business.

They are not really interested in facilitating your smooth transition into their country, they are only interested in their own little empire and giving you the run around.

Unless you're prepared to run the gauntlet with the wrong papers then all you can do is be patient, try and see the funny side crack on with other work you have and play the game, because it's just that, a game.

Making Friends and Allies

The longer you stay in a location the more you'll learn about it and the local **Do's** and Don'ts. By routinely being friendly, polite, cheerful and chatting to people you'll pick up little pieces of the picture. Such as areas that are off limits after dark because of the risk of muggings and rape. You won't be able to Google it, but they are most likely well known to the locals.

In Bosnia we got to know the neighbours on all sides of our house, we had BBQs in the summer and let the kids in to play with our Play Station. We dug out their cars in the winter while we were digging ours out. They liked us and we liked them, and on more than one occasion they warned us of impending trouble and when it came we were ready for it.

Be polite, respectful in all your dealings with absolutely everybody regardless of rank or station and you will win friend and allies where ever you go. Make an effort to learn people's names and greet them warmly when you see them, you'd be amazed at the effect you'll have if you make the effort to greet them by name. A smile costs nothing, it uses more muscles in your face to frown so make a point of smiling and you'll defuse tension wherever you go. Try it, it really works.

Mugging

You're walking back to your hotel and you hear footsteps gaining on you. The hairs on the back of your neck are standing on end and you think you're being followed and they're going to mug you. You should avoid unlit areas like parks, graveyards and short cuts after dark. Stay to the well-lit areas and if you can.

Ensure that you're walking confidently as if you have walked this road all your life, walk tall like you own the street. A survey of muggers and rapists serving prison time revealed that by and large they go for easy, opportunist victims. Girls who are wearing skirts, have long hair and don't look very confident give them encouragement that they will be easily able to drag them to the ground and assault/intimidate them.

He's Gaining on You

Confidently turning around and looking your unwanted shadow in the eye and saying "I've seen you and I know what you're doing, now get lost if you know what's good for you" takes some courage, but it might put him off, at the very least it'll show that you're not afraid of him.

He may walk past, look at you like you're crazy, but who cares? You can have a giggle about it later when you've calmed down and can see the funny side of it, you'll have taken control of the situation. Your attacker might be scared too, you might be his first.

Sad to say, but some men get a thrill out of scaring girls, they're not going to assault them but they will walk up behind them knowing that they are making them really nervous and get a buzz from it. Bullies are essentially weak individuals who take out their own feelings of inadequacy on those about them to make themselves feel better.

He's Still Following You

If he's still on your tail and you're only a short distance from your car/hotel, it might not be the safest place to go. Depending on your circumstance it might be better to head for a group of people, a restaurant, café or a well-lit area, even if you have to burst in to an open doorway. Throwing yourself on the good will of others.

"Hi, look I'm so sorry but I am being followed by someone and I'm really frightened" they'd have to be a very cold bunch to turn you away and not offer you refuge.

Talking on mobile phones can be very distracting normally, but it might be really useful here. Pull your phone out and talk loudly and confidently, whilst waving *"Simon, I'm over here at the end of the road, can you see me?"*

To give you an idea of just how distracting phones can actually be, a recent study concluded that a whopping 32% of road accidents during the school run in the UK were 11-12 year olds on their mobile phones. In the last 10 years almost 33,000 kids have been killed or seriously injured on our roads.

Weapons

If that's not worked and you're 100% that he's coming for you, then either prepare to run or prepare to fight. If you're going to run then kick off any heels you're wearing, drop your coat, bag or whatever else you're carrying (unless you can use it as a weapon, like a rolled up magazine, umbrella etc...) and go for your life. Head for a safe area, look behind you as often as you can, if he's catching you then could weave in and out of parked cars.

It sounds obvious but just do everything you can to prevent him from getting you on the ground, if there's obvious dark alleys then try and get as far from them as possible as this is probably where he'll try and drag you.

If you're going to fight then look around for anything that you can use to gain an advantage, gaining a bit of height might help, like a short set of steps at the entrance to someone's house. Get up them, hammer on the door and start yelling, then turn and face him. It's much better to turn and face him, it will give you a psychological advantage and it might deter him.

Dig into your pockets and get your keys in your hand, aim for the face, the throat and the genitals, no time for Queensbury rules here, bite, scratching, gouging and screaming are what's required.

Decide right from the start that you are not going to be taken down, go on the offensive, attack him with every bit of anger you can muster, show him no mercy because he won't show you any.

Robbers Wallet

If he's just after your wallet or your purse then having a robbers wallet to hand is ideal for giving him something, don't give it up too readily as he might smell a rat, stall him a bit make a bit of a show of getting it out and then offer it/throw it to him, he'll hopefully see the bundle of small denomination notes, think he's struck gold and run, leaving you to get to safety.

In Summary

- Save the drinking and merry making until you get home
- If you make a cultural gaff, apologise and mean it
- Ask hotel staff, cab drivers and colleagues about an area you're intending to visit, be inquisitive
- Let your colleagues know your plans, make sure your mobile is charged
- Expect to be followed in some countries, it is routine. But do not attempt to shake your tail the authorities won't find it in the least bit amusing
- Deal firmly with people trying to bribe you, ignore the casual attempts by passers-by. If it's an official ask to deal with it at the police station but be polite and reasonable
- Be friendly, make allies and talk to people wherever you go and you'd be amazed at how this will make your time easier
- Walk confidently and purposefully
- Keep to well-lit areas and use to your intuition, if it doesn't feel right then don't do it
- In areas where mugging is a problem carry a robbers wallet which you can hand over
- If you think a mugger/rapist is on your tail head for a well-lit busy area

13 ~ Vehicle Security

If you only take one thing away from this chapter, or are going to skip it entirely then **"Get to know your vehicle"**. Has it got a child lock in the rear, do the seat belts/air bags work, could you get out in a hurry? Travelling to Colombia ten years ago, what would have

"GET TO KNOW YOUR VEHICLE"

been your primary security concern? Most likely the fear of kidnap and then being held for ransom, or being caught up in a cross fire between the police and one of the drug cartels in Cali or Medellin. However ten years ago by far the biggest killer in Colombia (by a factor of 400%) was deaths in Road Traffic Collisions or RTCs.

RTCs in Nigeria are the third leading cause of death. According to the World Health Authority the country has 1,042 deaths for every 100,000 vehicles. The equivalent figures for the UK and US are 7 and 15. Bad roads bear some of the blame but appalling driving is the main reason, in April 2013 a bus driver trying to beat the curfew at 6pm crashed killing 20.

RTCs are not newsworthy or widely reported, they are routine wear and tear of life, a boring and run of the mill way to die that won't make the headlines, unless of course you're mega famous and then it's not about the fact that you died in a car, it's the personality.

In this week's Economist (at the time of writing in Jan 2014), an article states that there are now a staggering 1.3 million people killed each year from RTCs around the world, an incredible number.

Predictably the split between rich and poor countries is uneven, but entirely expected. In rich countries 99,000 die each year but in poor countries it's a whopping 1.2 Million per year.

Alcolock® GB DS-10.2

Restraints on drivers (speed limits, a culture of vehicle safety enforced by serious penalties) safety features in vehicles and investment in safety such as Alcolocks (that prevent you from driving if you're drunk) have contributed to making roads in places like America the safest since records began. Sweden is planning to make road deaths a thing of the past entirely.

But it's a very different story in poor countries. Developing countries see roads as a vital part of economic prosperity, they view deaths from RTCs are an inevitable cost, build the road quickly, get the economy going and then spend on safety measures later (when they get around to it, which they rarely do).

One sad fact is that it doesn't cost much to make these vital arteries of progress safe and the majority of the deaths are boys and working age men.

A maimed young adult can put a resource strain on a family that could potentially condemn it to poverty for between 2-3 generations.

The state of a country's roads is a consideration for you and your team when you deploy overseas for work. It's inevitable that you'll be a passenger or pedestrian for a proportion of your trip. So you need to keep your wits about you both on foot on the sidewalks and in the car.

The Driver

So what do you think the most dangerous part of the vehicle is? Tyres? Suspension? It's probably going to be your driver. If you were to ask a taxi driver in Truro at 11pm to drive you to John O'Groats 600 miles away, right at the end of his shift he'll shake his head and decline. It would be madness to undertake that fare and he'll suggest that he drives you to the station and you get a train.

But in some parts of the world where they simply couldn't contemplate turning down a chance to earn Western dollars, they won't even think twice. As you nod off in the back you've maybe got two hours before he does the same and you plummet into a ravine.

He might be drunk. The western world has a fairly clear cut policy on drink/driving and it has quite a stigma attached to it, but in countries where the police are on the take anyway and life is a bit cheaper generally you need to watch out, some drunks are masters at hiding it. The same with regular users of drugs.

An Unwelcome Visitor

He might not be welcome in the area that you're going to. Today's headlines are all about the problems in South Sudan and their neighbours in the Central African Republic. Two African nations rent in two by ethnic and tribal hatred so you'll need to be cautious about asking your

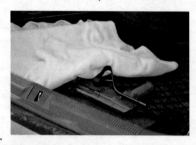

driver to take you to an area where his presence might put him and you in danger.

He might be carrying a weapon. Some organisations have a clear policy that they are to have nothing to do with weapons in or around their vehicles. Another company I trained deploying to Libya had armed guards and an escort, it's an assessment that you'll have to make on the ground **BUT** it's much better to know if your driver is armed before you set off.

The weapon might be discovered when your vehicle is searched and a young nervous guard gets excited and pulls the trigger on your driver because he's found a pistol in the glove compartment. So always ask him – "Are you carrying a weapon, can we see it please?" a good tactic is to use the approach "I'm sorry my friend, but it's our company policy, we have to check for our insurance and it's boring I know but we have to".

He Might Not Know Where he's Going?

I got a taxi to take me to a venue outside the city limits in Nairobi and it was only because I had done a map recce and kept me eye on the speedo that I realised he'd overshot and didn't know where the venue was. Despite nodding enthusiastically when we asked him several times that he definitely knew where it was. Some cab drivers don't know there way out of the city but will not say "No" to western travellers that tip much better than the local businessmen and who pay in US dollars.

So How Much do You Tell your Driver?

If he's a well trusted fixer/driver working for your organisation for a long time, a permanent employee, then you can be quite open about your destination, duration etc... Chances are he knows already because he got the schedule while you were still at home four weeks ago.

However if he's a completely new hire then you might need to be a little more cautious about giving him your complete itinerary in advance. Again you must use your intuition, if you tell him nothing about your destination then you won't be able to use his local knowledge to find out about the area you're visiting.

In Afghanistan we took Afghan National Army on joint patrols with us, we would tell our Afghan Army colleagues that we were taking them out for a patrol for 4 days, we would be leaving at this time and returning at this time but didn't reveal the destination til we set off.

Their ranks were occasionally compromised by the Taliban, we gave the guys enough information that they could prepare themselves for a 4 day patrol and pack their kit but that was all, we couldn't risk letting the Taliban know where we were going otherwise they would have arranged a reception for us.

Checking Over your Vehicle

It's not practical to check each vehicle from front to back each time you rent a cab. Taking a short cab ride in the city you can get away with a cursory external check (you can do this walking toward it, chatting to the driver, or as you see it pull up) we're familiar with this when we jump into our own car or that of a friend, we do it without even thinking about it.

But if you're taking a longer trip and farther afield then do a thorough check. If it's an all day trip then plan for an overnight stay, identify an area where you can overnight. Or at the very least take warm kit, a couple of sleeping bags in the boot. Just having the kit and having thought about it will be another mental box ticked, so you'll be more confident moving through your environment.

Jack and Spare Wheel

Get it all out, locate it, check the spare is inflated, check the jack, ensure it works and don't assume that the driver knows how to use it. If you have a flat on the road, far from aid you look at him accusingly, he looks at you "My cousin's car, not mine".

If you yell at him he might just take off and leave you. He'll be ok, probably got relatives nearby. It's a real pain when it all goes pear shaped but losing your temper and shouting doesn't help anyone.

The Safety nut on a wheel is designed to deter thieves, one nut on the wheel requiring a specific key located within the car tool kit, if it's missing you're not getting it off. A colleague fell foul of this along the Salang Highway in the Afghan winter and spent a cold uncomfortable night sharing a sleeping bag with his driver.

In Convoy

When driving in convoy with several other vehicles brief your driver/s on how you'd like them to drive. When you're out in the countryside and there's little threat you can have a decent distance between the cars. But when you're in town close the gaps and get as close as you can to prevent other vehicles pushing in between you and getting separated.

If you're using walkie talkies between vehicles, have them in the hands of a clear English speaker in both vehicles if possible, or two people who have similar accents that can understand one another. When talking on a radio think about what you're going to say before you press transmit, don't waffle and don't argue.

Remember to press the button wait a second and then talk. Nominate rendezvous points along the way that you can return to in case you get split up. When you pass an obvious rendezvous point, point it out to everyone, then have a look at it from the back window, that's the direction you'll be approaching from.

If you see something hazardous shout "Stop, Stop, Stop" they might not hear the first one but they'll hear the next two. Try and keep the speed down if you can, you can't outrun a bullet or a bomb but you can drive at a sensible speed, keep your eyes open and avoid driving into them. Also the faster you go the more dust and debris you'll kick up which will make it harder for the drivers behind you.

LPG Gas Bottles

In Islamabad, a journalist mentioned to me that a large number of cars in Pakistan are fitted with LPG fuel bottles, regarded as potential fire bombs in the back by many, they would insist that the driver empty it or they'd get another car without one.

There are two types of LPG bottle in the developing world, the imported ones from Europe and the US which are all kite marked and relatively safe, and the locally made knock off fakes which though considerably cheaper are deadly.

He told me of two separate incidents, one in which a vehicle rolled down a ravine and instantly burst into flames, the other reported a garage attendant who was ignorant of the correct level of the bottle and it exploded.

Another lady in Islamabad commented that in certain parts of Pakistan if you have a woman in the vehicle or children you are much less likely to be stopped, the locals are fiercely protective of families and kids and will whisk you through. If you have a vehicle which looks important, a land cruiser for example which is clean, well maintained then this can act in your favour, they will assume that you're someone of importance and not to be detained/ questioned.

How Do You Control your Driver?

He's not drunk, has had adequate sleep and he knows where he's going. He's not going to land you or himself in hot water because he's from a disliked group where you're heading. But not long into the journey you realise that he drives like a maniac and you're in fear of your life.

Initially try reasoning with him and say that you're afraid of the way he drives, tell him you want to see more of the countryside and take some photos but you can't because the countryside is passing by as a blur.

Blame your company's policy that invalidates insurance if you are in an accident in a country if you were exceeding the speed limit. Say you'll have to organise another taxi. You could try the one that I like best which is just to say you're feeling ill and will be sick if he doesn't slow down.

At the end of the day nobody wants to clear vomit up from the passenger foot well of their car no matter what a speed freak he is.

Carjacking

You're driving your "new" looking hire car around town, after a while you notice a vehicle in your rear view mirror with a couple of dodgy looking men that might be tailing you. Pulling up at a set of traffic lights, the hairs on the back of your neck standing up, you glance in the mirror and notice that there's now only the driver in the car behind you.

Before you can think about it, the door's wrenched open, you're tossed to the floor, your assailant swearing and cursing you are told to stay down and don't look up. With a roar and burning rubber the thief screams off leaving you prostrate on the tarmac. You've just been the victim of a carjacking.

Though often not fatal carjacking is a growing problem in parts of Nigeria, Pakistan, South Africa and Brazil. Weapons will often be brandished in your face but they are rarely after you personally, they're after the car which they will no doubt sell on - so don't look them in the eye, they will be more inclined to let you go if they know you won't be able to identify them.

Your safety and that of all the occupants is now your top priority, the car and your stuff is all replaceable as is your pride. Be very mindful of hot heads in the team, those with short tempers who might "kick off" and make the situation much, much worse. I have run scenarios before where we've had to stop people from belting one another.

- A question I am frequently asked is *"Is there such thing as a clean car, that won't get noticed?"* i.e. one that won't attract attention. The short answer is no not really, carjacking's are often entirely random incidents, so whatever you're driving that day, if someone can make some money from pinching it from you then they might just go for it. But you can try and drive a common looking car or one that won't look out of place amongst the flow of other traffic.

So what can you do to prevent this f rom happening?

Here are a few things to bear in mind.

- Always stay alert and be on the lookout for a tail, learn how to identify or confirm that you're being followed without actually alerting your shadow. Pulling into petrol stations, loop roads or roundabouts will confirm if they're after you. You can then either stay put or make for a busy area or a police station, hopefully they'll get bored waiting and move on to another target.

- Always leave enough room at the front of the vehicle to manoeuvre out of trouble if you find yourself boxed in. I always think to myself *"Wheels and Tarmac"*, if you can see those of the car in front of you, then you'll have room to swing out of the line of traffic either left or right.

- Assailants are often armed but in most incidents won't use them unless you provoke them. But don't forget they'll think nothing of knocking your teeth all over the road if you piss them off, so just don't chance it, don't get cocky or relax if they start to joke around with you, they might just be high or drunk and one smart arse move from you or grin might give them the excuse they are looking for to harm you. These guys are accustomed to violence, you are not.

- If you're going to be living and working in a remote area for a protracted period then you should consider taking a defensive driving course. Learn how to identify vulnerable points on the road such as long isolated stretches which should be avoided. Vary your travel routine and plan it in advance and make sure you log it with your bureau or colleagues, so they know where you were heading.

- Keep your eyes peeled and be aware of cars about you, try and avoid cars parked by the side of the road.

- Never stop at accidents or Road Traffic Collisions, it seems heartless but it might be a trap set for you. Don't offer people lifts either, it's just not worth it.

During a carjacking

You will probably be threatened with a weapon, try and remain calm and calm the more nervous members of the team, use slow calming tones when speaking, avoid any sudden movements which might antagonise your assailant. Move when/if they tell you to, be polite and answer questions truthfully if they ask you, your calm demeanour may well calm them down. Keep your hands in full view.

When You're Released

Don't look at them or the car and do exactly as they say.

In Summary

- Road safety in developing parts of the world is not what we're used to in the developed world, so extra care must be taken

- Get to know your vehicle, spend ten minutes learning how to get in and out, are there child locks in the back? Has it got a jack and spare wheel and are they correctly fastened and stowed? Familiarise yourself so you can get out in a hurry

- Road traffic collisions are a major cause of death and injury overseas

- Ensure your driver isn't either drunk, high, exhausted, a very fast driver or extremely unwelcome in the areas that you wish to visit

- Is your driver armed? Many people carry weapons routinely overseas and he might not even think to mention it

- Make your driver feel part of the team, but if he's a brand new hire don't feel you need to tell him absolutely everything

- If you're travelling in convoy nominate rendezvous points along the way that you can return to in case you get split up

- LPG bottles in some deprived parts of the world are cheap knock off's of the regulated models in the west. They are very dangerous and travel in these vehicles should be avoided

- If you want to slow your driver down and all other attempts have failed, tell him you're going to be sick. Nobody wants to clear up your vomit from their foot well, no matter how much he likes his speed

14 ~ Vehicle Check Points

Road blocks and Vehicle Check Points (VCPs) are easy to set up, flexible means of control common to many parts the world. Used by both official government forces and criminal and guerrilla groups to maintain a grip on an area.

They allow those running them to monitor movements of people and materials as well as to deny movement and disrupt their opponents. They are also a tool for bribery, extortion, kidnap and intimidation, sadly employed by both.

In some cases they are used to spread terror. Boko Haram militants operating in the north of Nigeria used fake Army checkpoints to flag motorists down. In the town of Logumami 19 residents had their throats cut as they wound down their windows. The latest in a string of atrocities by the group.

Temporary VCPs can be set up easily using a couple of cars on a highway with a handful of soldiers or thugs marshalling traffic. They can be erected in minutes and disappear as quickly.

Permanent VCPs are much larger, normally fortified positions that will consist of a traffic slowing obstacle like a chicane of barrels or concrete bollards, a fortified control position and a rest area for troops. There may be other sandbagged positions to cover the entrance and exits to the VCP.

What do They Want to Know?

1. Who you are

2. What you're doing

3. Where you've come from

4. Where you're going

In some parts of the globe bribery is on the agenda. In the Egyptian capital Cairo bribing traffic police officers is the norm. Low paid traffic cops view it almost as an unregulated informal way of supplementing their wages and everybody does it. Problems can arise in official as well as unofficial check points, they are all potentially hostile.

As a rule of thumb, in countries where the reach and influence of government is weak (because of the sheer size of the country or poor morale and discipline) then the risk of unofficial road blocks increases. Local forces feel that they have either been forsaken or they see it as an opportunity to profit from the instability.

Bribery Closer to Home than You Think

I was sitting in Webuyanycar.com selling my old heap a few weeks ago, chatting to the employee as he sorted my paperwork out. He told me he had recently returned from ten years living and working in Portugal.

It was a grey rainy day outside (little did we know that the rain wasn't going to stop for the next 4 weeks) and I joked that I bet he regretted it now eh?

> *"I couldn't afford to live their anymore, all the Brits and my colleagues from Germany and France we being stopped all the time by the cops and fined for fabricated offences, sometimes 2-3 times every day. Lots of us left."*

According to him, the European Union had spent a vast amount paying for a road to be refurbished, the Portuguese authorities then decided to plonk a toll station on it to charge motorists to use it. EU officials slapped their wrists with a huge fine, but they're still doing it because the revenues they get from the toll road eclipse the EU fine.

Where are They Located?

Normally positioned to protect certain areas, or to ensure you drive straight into them without having an opportunity to turn around, after a bend in the road, a forest track etc...

They might have a position on higher ground acting as an early warning which will have views to the rear and front. In Mexico some villagers, fed up with the murderous activity of the drug cartels, and the seeming inability of their government to protect them, have organised their own groups to control access to their communities.

They set up VCPs manned by armed villagers that monitor who comes in and out of their territory, search cars and have generally taken the law into their own hands.

This has inevitably led to running gun battles between the poorly trained and ill-disciplined locals and the sometimes highly trained and motivated drug gangs. Sadly some of the vigilantes have also succumbed to the temptation to abuse that power and extort bribes from those they profess to protect. Sometimes the temptation to abuse your position is too great.

What Kind of People Man VCPs?

Not the high flyers I'm afraid, no it'll be poorly paid, poorly educated foot soldiers. Their location and the standards of the local forces will be a litmus test of whether they are drunk, stoned, bored, poorly lead, ill disciplined, or all of the above.

They might be young, inexperienced and frightened too, or high on the power trip. The British Army has a deserved reputation for being a highly trained and disciplined force, but even within the British Army there are tales from VCPs that are less than exemplary. Soldiers occasionally muck about and if they're poorly led and paid it's even more likely.

They might be rather resentful that while they are stuck out in the cold or the heat with sod all to do, you've turned up in your air conditioned car with your ray-bans on looking cool, oozing purpose and privilege, expecting them to just wave you through.

Behaviour in the VCP

Keep quiet, be polite and don't get out of the vehicle unless you're ordered to. Exiting the vehicle without being told to turns it into a situation where you're forcing your protagonists to act, to save face, you've made an issue of it.

Things to Avoid

Involuntary smiling and nervous laughter. If you think this is you and you've a nervous disposition then don't sit in the front seat, or try and avoid talking to your protagonists. Leave it to the more confident member of the group. Keep calm and don't raise your voice or show them you're pissed off or aggravated. Look them in the eye, wearing sun glasses is just rude.

Your Approach to the VCP

Keep the doors locked and your hands where they can see them. Pass messages to one another, keep the commentary going so that you all know what's happening, and keep your eyes peeled, all round observation.

Before you set off talk through with the team and your driver what you'll do in the event of a VCP. Nominate a spokesman and make sure you are all singing off the same hymn sheet in terms of why you're all there. Nominating a female boss can make life easier in some African countries, but cause you problems in some Islamic Countries.

When driving into a VCP bear in mind that you don't know what might have happened recently. These guys might have been in gunfights literally hours before you arrived, they might be twitchy, and feel that they are well within their rights to open fire.

When you see a VCP ahead slow down but don't slam on the breaks, look around for instructions on sign posts and from the soldiers and obey them. If you come across the VCP by surprise don't reverse out at speed, finish conversations and put your phones away carefully without making sudden moves. Talk calmly to one another and about what's going on, this will soothe the nerves of the more nervous team members.

Do not film as you're driving in, in fact just stop doing anything at all that might annoy them, or give them cause to detain you.

A Pakistani journalist that I taught a few years ago related an incident where she had come around the corner from a night with friends straight into a VCP. She quickly turned off her lights and reversed at speed in a dramatic squeal of burning rubber, and they had all opened fire on her.

I asked her if she'd do the same thing if it happened again she said she would, she couldn't grasp the idea that her actions might have prompted them to open fire in the first instance by acting like a car full of criminals rather than a legitimate civilian going about her business. If one person starts firing, they all will.

What Will they Want?

Unless they just waive you through, they'll probably ask you where you're going, who's in the vehicle, who's in charge? What you're doing? They might just want to inconvenience you, or perhaps extract a trophy, some sort of one-upmanship, to demonstrate that they are in charge.

Without capitulating entirely it will help you to give them that impression for now. Let them have their little victory, it means little to you does it? They might just want a bribe, so find out how much is an acceptable amount, you don't want to insult them but you don't want to get fleeced either.

If they are scrutinising your documents and have been for some time without letting you pass on, you could suggest *"If we don't have the correct passes, is there maybe a day permit that we could purchase from you?"* At the end of the day you'll save face for both sides and can return through the VCP later with little ill feeling.

Don't hand over your passport, you might not see it again, or they might just be trying to use it to get you out of the car, to follow them into their guard hut. Keep your

passport hidden in your money belt, in your pocket, or somewhere that's easy to access.

Instead of handing over your passport, keep a couple of laminated copies of your ID or passport that you can hand over instead, that way if it is taken you can drive off and leave it. But don't try and get on a plane with your laminated copy by mistake.

The Language Barrier

Whose problem is it if they can't understand you? It's yours! Language barriers can be overcome by keeping your responses simple and answering only when spoken to, it's likely the first question will be *"Where are you going?"* You don't need to give a long reply.

If you're nervous and talk too much this may well make your questioner feel ignorant because he can't understand you. So just keep it really simple (nearest town) hotel, use gestures, bed, hotel and point, same as where you've come from.

What if They Haven't got Weapons on Display?

If a bunch of idle kids are manning a VCP with sticks and machetes, not in uniform and looking a bit ragtag, chances are they won't have anything bigger in the bushes covering you.

If they did they'd probably have it on show, you don't always have to stop. If you don't want to get involved then you can sometimes drive through carefully and slowly or drive around it.

Your local fixer will know how to handle most Circumstances if you're fortunate enough have one, so it's important to chat things through with him and the rest of the team before you depart. If you tell him to stop at every single VCP and let you do the talking then that's exactly what he'll do. But if you give him a bit of leeway and ask him for his advice he'll most likely be able to handle the situation.

Cover Story

If you decide to use a cover story make sure that you all know it back to front, and don't forget to involve your local driver. Don't make it complicated, if it's as close to the truth as practical it'll be a lot easier to remember, especially if you're under pressure.

Also bear in mind that when you employ a driver his presence may cause you problems as well. If he's from a disliked sect/tribe/group you might be in trouble, the least of all being that you'll get no further, you can't leave him behind.

Getting Out of the Vehicle

Try and avoid getting out if you possibly can, and certainly don't exit the vehicle unless instructed. It might be seen as a challenge especially if you're a taller than your protagonist. By staying in the car you haven't escalated the situation, it is contained and you're no threat to his ego. He can then let you go without losing face which will be a whole lot simpler.

But if you get out of the vehicle either invited or not, you have made a situation where there wasn't one before. He's now got to demonstrate a reason for getting you out, he'll search you, open the trunk, maybe get the others out and start questioning the driver too.

If you're ordered to *"Get out!!"* once, you might ignore it and try and humour him, see if you can sort the problem out without getting out. But if he says it again and looks like he's getting pissed off and starts yanking at the door you may have to do what he says. If

weapons get cocked and levelled at you and the vehicle then you have little choice but to do exactly what he says.

Getting Separated

Up to now you've been compliant and accepted what's happening to you. But if they try and take one of the group away, it's at this stage that you should dig your heels in. You mustn't lose sight of any of the group, especially not females and at night.

Within seconds your colleague could be beyond your help and whisked away. Offer to go all together, plead with them, tell them that you're frightened, that he/she is frightened.

Boring Dinner Party Guest

VCPs are often manned by your classic school bully type, so the approach I usually take if I have to talk to the soldiers is to act like the most boring dinner party guest ever (I have to work really hard at it obviously, because I'm incredibly good company – tongue firmly in cheek). Picture yourself at a party, you introduce yourself to the guy on your left and very quickly you're thinking *"Oh No, I've got a couple of hours stuck with him!!!"*

You can't just turn your back on him, but he's an expressionless, unexciting individual with nothing much to say for himself, he doesn't really laugh at your jokes, he doesn't have much of an opinion about anything, shows little interest in you and says almost nothing about himself, replying with "Yes" or "No" to your charming repartee. What a dull bloke, awful at a dinner party, but fantastic in a VCP.

In Summary

- Vehicle Check Points all have the potential to be dangerous and should be approached with great care
- They're not manned by the high fliers, but often by bored, ill-disciplined and paid or even drunk troops
- They'll want to know who, what, where to and where from?
- They are a focal point for extortion and intimidation, used to funnel traffic and to control the population
- Soldiers and Police manning VCPs are sometimes vulnerable because they are static in one location. If they've been attacked before they may be very twitchy
- Once one person starts firing they all will, so be very slow and deliberate in your movements
- Keep quiet, be polite and don't lose your temper
- Don't wear sunglasses when talking in the VCP, it's just rude
- Keep your hands where they can see them and your answers short and clear, don't elaborate
- The language barrier is your problem not theirs
- If you have to use a cover story make sure everyone including your driver is well versed and make it as close as possible to what you're actually doing
- Don't get out unless you have to
- Don't allow team members to be lead away or separated

15 ~ Weapons

Why do Men Carry Guns?

Because guns are cool – They confer authority, make young men feel tough, threatening, empowered and fearless. They allow the dis-enfranchised to get what they want, they give the carrier a respect, that's why people carry them. But the injuries they inflict stay with the injured person for the rest of their lives, if not ending it there and then.

Weapons are dangerous enough in the hands of highly trained uniformed soldiers, as part of an official sanctioned accountable armed force. The risks are compounded when weapons are placed in the hands of individuals who are accountable to no one, have little hope or anything to live for, are out for themselves, crazed by ideology, drunk and drugged.

Innocent people are killed around the world each year because of mistaken identity, misunderstanding, fatigue, fear, resentment, rogue elements or jealousy. And accidents happen, weapons however don't discharge themselves, the triggers are pulled by people.

In this chapter we'll look in some detail at -
- Different types of weapons
- Some popular myths
- Your best defence
- Cover from Fire and View

Different Types of Weapons

The world is awash with weapons, they're being produced almost as quickly as they're being decommissioned, taken off the streets and destroyed. Some are easily recognised and iconic like the AK47 and the M16 and some are weird and exotic homemade

weapons that are sometimes as much a danger to the firer as the intended target. Too numerous to list them all, below is a list of the main categories

- Grenades
- Hand guns / pistols
- Shotguns
- Assault Rifles / Carbines
- Submachine guns
- Sniper Rifles
- Machine guns
- Mortars

Broadly speaking they are split into two categories 1. **Heavy Weapons** and **2. Small Arms.** Looking at the list above small arms are man portable and lightweight, getting heavier as you go down the list to Machine guns. We're then into the heavy weapons which as the name suggests are heavy and need more than one person to carry them such as a Heavy Machine gun to Tanks and Artillery that are either self-propelled or on their own special trailer with a crew to operate them.

Do they All Work the Same Way?

No, they all throw projectiles at you with varying degrees of accuracy, some explode but most don't. The two types of delivery are Direct and Indirect Fire. A pistol for example is direct fire weapon, the firer can see you and points the weapon directly at you and he can see you through the sights, Bang – Ouch!

A mortar on the other hand which is at the other end of the list is an Indirect fire weapon, the firer can't actually see you through the weapons sights (he could be as much as 5 kilometres away) and he's probably acting on instructions from another person nearby who is feeding him coordinates and directions.

He adjusts his dials, pops the mortar in the big tube and covers his ears. "Boom" as it flies out of the tube and over the mountain or hillside in your direction, followed by some whistling and a crash as it explodes. Tanks, artillery and rockets are also indirect fire weapons due to the great ranges they are capable of.

Grenades

A hand grenade is a small explosive charge encased in
a metal jacket or wrapped in tightly woven steel wire.
Thrown either by hand or fired from an under slung
grenade launcher (UGL) beneath a rifle barrel.

Grenades can be thrown about 25 metres by a skilled
soldier but if fired from a UGL it can hit targets out to
400 metres or more.

If you're on boggy ground or in a cultivated area some
of the killing force of the explosion will be dissipated and
absorbed by the boggy ground. But if you in a narrow
street on a metalled road then the fragments will bounce
off walls and hard surfaces. If you're within 15 metres of a
grenade when it goes off you'll be seriously hurt or killed
and these splinters and fragments can go out to 200
metres from the detonation point.

There are number of different types of grenades from
stun grenades (lots of light and noise – non lethal), smoke
grenades which designed to mask movement around the
battlefield or to indicate an area like a helicopter landing

site. White/red phosphorous (very nasty – burning incendiary) and high explosive anti-personnel.

Contrary to what you see in the movies 99% of hand grenades do not explode on impact, they have an internal timing fuse which is started as soon as it leaves the hand of the thrower. A small spring loaded lever flies off and you've got between 5-10 seconds to seek cover. There won't be any smoke coming from it as the fuse burns internally.

Occasionally grenades don't go off, something has gone wrong inside and it just lies there, but don't sigh "Phew" just yet, it is still deadly and could go off at any second, so remain flat on the floor and crawl to the nearest hard cover and stay low.

If you are caught out in the open with no hard cover like ditched or walls to hide behind, try and lower your profile, do not attempt to flee too far. Hit the ground on your front and cover your head with your arms. It sounds counter intuitive to point your head toward the explosion but your arms should protect it, pointing your body towards the grenade and not at 90 degrees to it will mean the rest of your body is hidden.

When the grenade has gone off your ears will be ringing like crazy (if you can hear at all at this point) and your body will be coursing with adrenaline, try and muster what grit and determination you have within you and make your way to safety. Keep your eyes peeled for other threats too, some grenades are extremely powerful and can weaken structures which might collapse after it's gone off.

Hand Guns - Pistols

Pistols come in a range of models, normally firing 9 mm ammunition which as you can see on the image is a short stubby little round, not designed to go great distances. With a magazine capacity of up to 13 rounds a pistol's effective range (the range at which it would kill someone) is about 40 metres.

Anything beyond 40 metres and it'll hurt like bloody hell, might break bones and knock you over and may even break the skin.

But due to the round not being very aerodynamic or having a lot of gunpowder "Ooomph" behind it, it will have slowed down considerably and probably will not kill you, unless of course it strikes you directly in the temple in which case it just wasn't your day I'm afraid.

9 mm ammunition (sub-sonic, low velocity) is also used in sub machine guns, favoured by Security Forces protecting airports and vulnerable facilities where there are lots of civilians. The bullet enter the body, flattens or squashes out and stays in there.

Rifle ammunition (super-sonic or high velocity) on the other hand, travels through the body ricocheting about off bones and often comes out of the other side of your body to kill or wound someone else.

9 mm ammunition is the London bus to the 7.62 or 5.56mm rifle ammunition's Ferrari.

Shotguns

A shotgun is normally a long barrelled weapon (unless it's been sawn off to make it easier to conceal in a car or under a coat) they fire a range of different cartridges as you can see in the image. The cartridge at the top is a non-lethal round which is basically a silicon filled bean bag designed to bring someone down without drawing blood or breaking bones.

The cartridge below that is an example of normal shotgun ammunition. Filled with steel or lead ball bearings or "shot" (hence the name shotgun) shotguns are designed for game shooting not combat and hence their effective range is limited to something like 30 metres.

The bottom cartridge is called a "slug" and is a solid single shot, like one large ungainly bullet. Used historically for breaching doors by shooting off the hinges and locks, it is not used much anymore because it would go through the door and bounce around the room potentially harming innocents within. Modern breaching cartridges are filled with silicon or sand which does a lot of damage to the door but would quickly lose much of its kinetic, killing energy.

Submachine Guns

Submachine guns or SMGs are basically pistols with long barrels and larger magazines, they are the middle step between a pistol and an Assault Rifle. Submachine guns have a bigger magazine capacity and can normally hold 30 rounds, unlike pistols they can fire on fully automatic. Pull and hold the trigger and it will fire all the rounds in the magazine, as well as single shots and small bursts of 3-4 rounds.

With the longer barrel comes a longer range and greater accuracy, this is derived from the fact that it is normally fired from a stable position in the shoulder and the greater range from the longer barrel. Effective range is out to 50 metres.

Using 9mm pistol ammunition, SMGs are favoured by SWAT teams and Police Forces when operating in densely populated areas.

Assault Rifles / Carbines

Assault rifles are probably the most common weapon around, they are sometimes referred to as Personal Weapons or Individual weapons because they are sighted to an individual soldier's body shape, his height, length of his arms etc... So if another soldier picked it up and fired a weapon other than his own, he wouldn't be as accurate had he fired his own weapon sighted to him.

Assault Rifles use a longer, sleeker round than the short stubby 9mm round in pistols, they are designed to kill at ranges out to 600 metres. Although gun battles and ambushes these days in Afghanistan take place at ranges nearer 100 – 200 metres.

The two rifle rounds that you can see in the image are 5.56mm used by the British Army (and many of its NATO allies in their different weapons) and the 7.62mm which is used in the AK47 common to Russian Forces and their client states. AK47s are also used widely by terrorist and insurgent forces.

Assault rifles have a magazine which holds up to 30 rounds, soldiers typically will carry between 5-6 magazines each, they very are accurate in the hands of a skilled marksman. Fired with the butt placed firmly in the shoulder, supported by two hands and sometimes a tripod makes for increased accuracy. As a rule of thumb the longer the barrel the longer the range.

We'll explore types of cover at the end of the chapter.

Sniper Rifles

In the previous paragraph on Assault Rifles I mentioned that the longer the barrel the greater the range and accuracy. Sniper Rifles have the longest barrels of all small arms. This increased accuracy is derived from the skills of the Sniper in the art of shooting, the advanced optical sights fitted to sniper weapons and the very high grade of ammunition that they use.

The science bit behind the long barrel is thus: inside the barrel there are a number of tiny grooves that twist all the way down the barrel.

As the bullet travels down the barrel these grooves make the bullet spin. The longer the barrel the more it spins and the more it spins the more stable the flight of the bullet which makes it much more accurate.

Picture an American Football Quarterback throwing the ball to one of his team mates running ahead of him to the touch line.

He draws his arm back and puts that characteristic spin on it which means it's accurate (it goes to the right player) with much increased range. Picture him throwing like a girl with his other arm and it wouldn't go very far would it?

Not everyone that carries a Sniper Rifle however will be a sniper, or might not be as highly trained as the individual who sports the coveted sniper badge of the British Army.

With every passing month the range of sniper weapons is increasing as technology introduces new materials and techniques. In November 2009 a British Army Corporal killed 2 Taliban Insurgents at a range of 2,475 metres an astonishing range which is over 1.5 miles.

Machine Guns

Machine guns are carried by one man, but this soldier normally has a colleague called a No2 who helps him to spot the enemy, directing him onto the position and also to carry extra ammunition. Unlike the other weapons that we have looked at, Machine guns do not use magazines, they use bullets joined together with small links which is referred to as a "Belt" of ammunition.

Machine guns as you can see in the image are fitted with a bi-pod, this enables the firer to lie on the ground and have the barrel lifted out of the grass/ dirt so that he just has to shift his position a bit to bring the weapon onto the target. By pulling the gun into his shoulder and achieving a firm solid firing position the machine gunner can put down a deadly and accurate amount of fire.

Machine guns can fire up to 750 rounds a minute (which is a frightening 12 rounds per second) if it's fired by a soldier on his belly he will be able to hit targets out to 800 metres. However if he fits it to a large, heavy, solid tripod which is steadied by sandbags (this is called the Sustained Fire roll) he can hit targets out to 1800 metres.

Mortars

We are now into the realm of the Indirect Fire weapons systems (when the firer can't actually see his intended victim, because it's too far away or behind an obstacle). Mortars are capable of sending a projectile almost 6 kilometres, there are various different types of rounds from High Explosive, fragmentation to Incendiary and smoke which are used to blind enemy to the advance of troops.

Mortars consist of a base plate (on which the tube stands), the tube itself and the tripod that the tube rests against. A mortar is normally carried in a vehicle but it can be man packed across terrain by 3 soldiers although this is a quite a task. A few examples of the projectiles that are fired can be seen in the photograph.

The projectile (or bomb as it's referred to) is placed at the head of the tube and released so that it slides down the tube. It strikes the percussion cap at the bottom which sends the mortar back up the tube and away to its target in much the same way as an arrow fired a long distance it will ark through the air. It does not have any propulsion as say a rocket or missile would once its flying it's beyond any form of control from the firer.

Mortars in the hands of the untrained operator can be wildly inaccurate and it is for this reason that so many innocents are killed by them in conflict areas. Fired in the rough direction of an enemy position they can fly further on or fall short.

Unlike tanks and artillery that are preceded by a characteristic loud report or explosion at the position of firing, mortars can sound like a very faint "Crump" even in the open. But if you are in a built up area you may very well not hear anything at all. Mortars will make a whistling sound as it approaches the ground but by the time you hear that it may very well be too late and all you can do it "Hit the dirt".

Rockets – Artillery – Tanks

I am not going to waste your valuable time by describing Rockets, Artillery and Tanks in detail because I would much rather you read all the other useful stuff in this book (or admired the exquisite graphics). All you need to know is what to do when they start landing around you. Essentially they all do the same thing, all that differs is

how they do it. Rockets are long aerodynamic tubes packed with explosives, they can reach out to 50-60 kms. Artillery pieces are towed behind trucks and fire enormous bullets called shells which they can fire out to ranges in excess of 17 kms. Lastly Tanks are basically artillery pieces on a mobile platform which can engage and kill other tanks at 6 kms. The reason they are called Tanks is because during WW1 when they were being invented it was so top secret that even the people building them were led to believe that they were water tanks.

Some Popular Myths

Bullets by and large don't explode, and not everyone that fires a gun is going to hit you, even someone who's had a whole load of training and years of experience.

An FBI agent was following a drug dealer in the US a few years ago, the dealer walked into an elevator and the agent followed him in. So there they were in the elevator with one other person a woman, the dealer spots the covert ear piece in the agent's ear and pulls his pistol out.

The agent draws his out and they start shooting at each other, up to 26 bullets are fired in that lift, how many do you think hit flesh? Not one, they were shooting wildly and probably with their eyes closed.

Your Best Defence

- Knowledge
- Distance
- Hard Cover
- Not being there

Knowledge – As I have said several times already "knowledge is power". Knowledge of the characteristics and ranges of weapons will help you make an assessment and chose a course of action.

For example if some guy is waving a pistol at you from 300 metres away and shouting at you to "stand still, hands up" and you really don't want to comply and you're in a car.... Then you have some options open to you, you don't have to freeze and wait the couple of minutes til he gets to you, you can drive off. Even if you're on foot, he's not going to be able to hit you from that range.

Distance – Bullets and splinters from grenades and mortar rounds lose their lethality the further away you get from the firer and from the explosion, they slow down as the energy propelling them wears out. So if you can't remember the safe distances or ranges of weapons or can't make out what kind of weapon it was, then just get as much distance between you and him as you can.

It takes an experienced, skilled combat marksman about 5-6 seconds to shoot accurately at an opportunity target that pops up. He sees you, he identifies you as his quarry and he raises his weapon, steadies himself, gets you in his sights and takes the shot.

"I'm up, I am running, he's seen me, I'm down"

Have this mantra in the back of your head as you're sprinting from hard cover to hard cover no more than about 4 seconds, it'll seem like a lot longer when you're up believe me.

Hard Cover – Exactly what it says on the tin, getting yourself behind something that bullets won't penetrate. An interesting fact, in Sweden during Arctic Warfare training the soldiers are taught to compact 2 metres of snow in front of their chilly positions because this will stop a bullet from an Assault rifle.

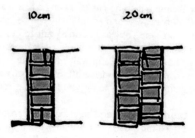

A single thickness brick wall of 10 cm might stop a pistol round, if it was fired from 30 metres or so away, but it would not stop an assault rifle round. However a double thickness brick wall of 20 cm thickness would stop a bullet from an assault rifle, but if the same bricks were to take a few rounds one after the other eventually they would penetrate.

If you are caught out in the open with no hard cover behind which to hide, try and lower your profile, you'll be much harder to hit with a bullet and be much safer from shrapnel and flying debris. Hit the ground on your front and cover your head with your arms.

Once you're on the ground get your head up cautiously and look around quickly for your next bit of hard cover to run to.

Not being there – By far the best defence against any kind of weapon or munition is just not to go anywhere near them or the people that wield them. Is the trip/ task really worth you personally going there, could you not send a local employee who is far less likely to arouse suspicion and knows the area much better than you?

This however is not always achievable if you are overseas and in an area where they proliferate. If you adhere to the lessons and principles in this book (or even better attend one of our HASP courses) you'll know to keep asking questions about the areas you're going to. Retain that childlike inquisitiveness and keep your eyes and ears open.

16 ~ Mines

Mines and Booby Traps

If you don't know what an IED is, then you have had your head buried firmly in the sand for the last decade or more. The threat of Improvised Explosive Devices (IED) faced by soldiers around the globe and are as much of a threat to civilians and travellers who stray off the beaten track.

Mines, bombs and artillery shells and other such materiel of war all contain explosives that terrorists find on the battle field or acquire from corrupt governments.

Colonel Muammar Gadaffi the now deceased leader of Libya, used to buy Semtex legally claiming it was for commercial mining but sell it to IRA in Northern Ireland to wage their campaign against the British. Insurgents and criminal groups get hold of the explosives, remove it from

Improvised Explosive Device (IED)

its casing and mould it into a form that they can conceal near their intended target, such as a kerb stone.

A common way of removing the explosives is to boil the shell until the explosive is in a more liquid form and then poor it out.

Why Mines?

Mines were widely employed throughout historical conflicts, and much of the developing world is still littered with them. Referred to as "Legacy Munitions" or Explosive Remnants of War (ERW), mines were designed to delay advancing troops, protect their flanks and likely approach areas.

To disrupt and channel military formations into killing zones, the unseen lurking threat of mines is a potent fear inducer, and will have a detrimental effect on morale on an advancing force.

Mines don't need feeding, they don't need to be relieved and they will cover a soldier's flank when he is asleep. But they are also indiscriminate, they kill and injure both friend and foe, this includes women, kids, livestock and young men and women. Once these youngsters have been maimed they will not only have been removed from the working capital of the nation, but be an intolerable burden on a family and condemn it to further poverty.

Mines are also used to protect flanks as part of a defensive position and to create a nuisance obstacle to delay troops, they are often covered by machine gun or sniper fire. Other types of minefield might be a "dummy one" where there aren't any mines just the surface signs, they'll know about it but you won't, this might be a marked escape route for the enemy.

Legacy Munitions

Many of the areas that are today littered with mines were laid years ago, during conflicts that are long since over, and the armies departed. When they were laid they should have been clearly marked on maps and charts, but many were never marked, or the charts lost.

The mine fields then became just as much of a threat to those that laid them, as to their enemies and to the civilian population that had to return and work the land when the fighting moved on.

There are millions of Legacy munitions scattered across the globe and at the present painstaking rate of clearing up, it will take almost a hundred years to be rid of them. That would be a depressing enough statistic on its own if it weren't for the fact that they are still being laid today.

Mine types

Mines fall broadly into two categories

1. **Anti Personnel (AP)** which are about the size of a tin of tuna or a tin of beans, designed to maim and injure rather than kill, although they very often do.

2. **Anti tank/ vehicle (AT)** designed to destroy / immobilise tanks and vehicles.

There are too many types and variants of mine to list in this book, so I have listed a few types to give you an idea how they function.

Much of the damage, done to the lower limbs from AP mines is from the blast itself, with additional injury from the metallic casing that it's housed in. The blast pics up debris and turns into whirling shrapnel which can include stones, soil, nuts, bolts, glass in fact anything that's lying around.

The devastating power of explosives is the speed at which the plasticine like material is transformed almost instantly into a cloud of gas, carrying everything with it and transforming everyday objects into deadly shrapnel. To illustrate this imagine a block of explosive about the size a standard bar of cheese from the supermarket in a warehouse.

Lying around the warehouse are a couple of bicycles, some old tables and chairs covered in cups and saucers, a computer and lots of the other stuff that we live with. When the explosive bar is set off it would instantly fill the warehouse with explosive gas and swirling objects doing the most appalling damage to anyone within.

Anti-Personnel (AP) Mines

There are a number of different types of AP mines - blast, fragmentation, directional and bounding.

Blast Mine

A typical off the shelf Blast mine is a small plastic, or non-metal construction nowadays to defeat metal detection) mine like the PMN. Once laid in position it will have the firing pin removed and a small acid pellet will eat through a retaining spring which will arm the mine, allowing the layer to get clear.

Foot pressure will initiate it and the blast will tear through the lower limb usually requiring amputation.

These mines if not recovered and destroyed, can lay for years waiting for an unlucky victim.

They commonly move about as soil is disturbed during cultivation and can be washed down slopes, into rivers, and even tilled by tractors etc... Once laid they are all but impossible to defuse or make safe unless done so by an EOD (Explosive Ordnance Disposal) or de-mining professional.

Fragmentation

POMZ-2 is a stake-mounted, anti-personnel fragmentation mine. An explosive charge wrapped into metal casing or a container that resembles a bar of chocolate. Designed to fracture and whip out as deadly shrapnel when the device functions it is placed on a stake stuck in the ground at about knee height in cover. A trip wire will run across the track or path and be triggered by soldiers walking by.

The body of the mine is a cast-iron thick-walled tube with six rows of cast fragmentation "chunks" and is usually painted olive green. The wooden stakes may be green, brown or unpainted.

Bounding Fragmentation

OZM-4 is a metallic bounding fragmentation mine, command or trip wire detonated. Usually found with a trip or trailing wire, a loose wire that will get caught on boots and shoes and pulled as you walk by setting off the mine. A bounding fragmentation mine will usually kill the person who sets it off and injure anybody nearby by the propelling fragments.

The cylindrical mine body is located in a short pot or barrel, which is buried in the ground. Tripping the wire detonates a smaller explosive charge in the base of the pot, which propels the mine body upwards.

As it "bounds" into the air to the height of approx. 0.5 a metre, the mine is activated by a thin cable secured to the barrel assembly. The cable pulls a pin from the bottom of the mine much like a grenade. The resulting blast scatters fragments, some of which may be preformed, over a much wider radius if it had been on the ground, as it will be free of surrounding obstacles like bushes, grass etc...

A colleague of mine had a very near miss with one of these mines, whilst walking across the Iraqi border at the beginning of the first Gulf War. He clipped the trailing wire with his boot and the device functioned, whilst he was standing directly above it. As the pot flew into the air it hit the bottom of his weapon and dropped harmlessly to the ground.

He then spent the next 4 hours motionless above this mine while the Bomb Squad were called, the rest of his colleagues having retreated a safe distance back so they wouldn't be harmed if it went off.

Directional AP Mine

MON-50 is a Soviet version of the American M-18 Claymore, a directional fragmentation mine. The curved base plate is filled with ball bearings or short steel rods depending on the variant in front of the explosive charge. It is usually sited backed against a tree or other hard surface to force the pellets fwd into the designated killing area.

Sometimes described as the military equivalent of an enormous sawn-off shotgun, the widely copied American M-18 Claymore mine contains 700 steel balls and can kill targets up to 50 metres away. Other types can kill people as far away as 200 metres. Directional fragmentation mines can be victim intiated or by command wire.

PFM-1 "Butterfly Mine"

Butterfly mines are responsible for lots of casualties among children. Rumour has it that the mine was deliberately designed to attract children, but in reality the mine's shape was dictated by aerodynamics.

Deployed aerially both from helicopters and aircraft, it would literally float to the ground. Due to its unusual shape and colouring, green, grey and white, the mine was often mistaken for toys by children who would throw

them in the air to watch them fly, or throw them at one another. Upon exploding, it often resulted in hand and head trauma.

The mine is basically a plastic bag containing explosive liquid, squeezing the soft plastic skin of the mine forces the arming plunger to strike the detonator detonating the mine. The mine is stored with a pin restraining a detonating plunger. The arming pin is removed just before they are deployed, the plunger is slowly forced by a spring forward until it contacts the detonator, at which point it is armed.

AT Mines

Anti-tank mines are designed to damage or destroy large military and civilian vehicles. A common tactic is to target the tracks so as to immobilise the vehicle, possibly as part of an ambush which would then be followed up by small arms fire to target the stationary vehicles behind.

Compared to Anti-Personnel mines Anti-Tank mines have a much larger explosive charge inside the body. They are equipped with a fuse designed only to be triggered by vehicles or, in some cases, tampering with the mine.

Many old AT mines were housed in wooden cases, with time the wood perished and disappeared entirely, the consequence of this is that the old AT mine which used to have an initiating pressure of 300 kg, now has one as little as 5 or 6 kg, turning AT into a massive AP.

Modern developments in AT mines have seen different, more powerful explosive payloads, plastic being used in construction to make them harder to detect with metal detectors. Shaped charges being employed that focus the power to penetrate the armour and sophisticated anti tamper devices that target the EOD teams.

You Encounter a Mine or Mine Field

You're in a vehicle in a convoy that's accidentally driven off the road, one of the vehicles in the front has hit a mine and there's a huge explosion and your car is showered with soil, gravel and debris.

When your ears stop wringing and you calm down you spot mine signs, but too late. Or you might have wandered off the road and suddenly you spot something in the grass!! What would you do?

If you're on foot, freeze and shout **"STOP, STOP, STOP!!!"** and make sure everyone hears you, ensure that the message gets passed to everybody. You need to let everyone know and do it forcefully. Your objective is now to make your way back very slowly to a metalled road or hard standing.

If you are in a vehicle do not be tempted to reverse out using the tracks that you vehicle has made. Unless you're the Stig you won't be able to do it accurately enough to guarantee you won't trigger it. Furthermore you may have driven over a double impulse device which will function at the second pressure. These are designed to allow a vehicle to pass over it and function when the rest of the column are well into the minefield.

"STOP!!! STOP!!! STOP!!!"

Look, Feel and Prod

Look down at your feet, not a cursory glance but a proper scan, you're looking for things that shouldn't be there, anything suspicious. There are very few straight lines in nature so look for straight edges of the casing, or the smooth shining curves. Once you've identified it leave it alone, do not be tempted to "over confirm" either, mark it if you can with whatever you have to hand, or if you can't ensure that the guy behind you knows about it and he passes that along to the guy behind him and so on.

Keep the communication going, it will calm everybody down a bit. Start by clearing an area for your feet, ensure that it's big enough for both feet with a bit of room to spare as well. You may have to crouch down, so give yourself some wiggle room, and remember there's no rush, take your time and do it thoroughly.

It's tiring and painstaking work, so make sure you clear enough room so that you can drop onto one knee if you need to. When you've cleared it then you need to mark it, the best method is mine tape, but if you don't have that then improvise, but ensure you mark it clearly.

You then need to start clearing your route back to a known safe area or hard standing, via the shortest path possible. Carefully clear an area about the size of a packet of cigarettes or a pack of cards by sliding your prodder at 45 degrees over your knuckles.

You go in from this angle to ensure you don't prod the top of the mine and set it off. Clear one small area then clear around it until you've cleared an area that you can squat in and put your knee down. In this fashion you can clear a series of stepping stones of safe ground back to a known clear area or hard standing.

Local Warning Signs

The native population won't have access to official mine signs, so they'll improvise, and you need to be able to spot them. Painted rocks (red points to danger - white to a safe area) or piles of stones might well mark dangerous areas. Local people particularly in poor areas need the land in order to survive, they graze there cattle and livestock on it as well as growing crops.

They live and work on the land and will know from bitter experience where the danger areas are. You may well notice amputees in the area, children with a hand missing or scarring to the face, men on crutches.

Absence of the normal, presence of the abnormal.
All the things that you see as you're on the road, coupled
with your background research and talking to the locals
should alert you to the presence of danger. Craters,
dead livestock left out to
rot in the fields, signs of
damaged vehicles, scars
of war.

Crossed sticks with cans
or bottles on them, are
a common local warning,
lines of stones along a
pathway, in fact anything
that looks like it's been
placed there for a reason,
usually has been, so take
care.

If in doubt don't walk or drive off the metalled road
(Tarmac), however if a track looks well used and you can
see locals going up and down it then it might be ok.

Bear in mind though that due to some countries living
with death/disfigurement and years of civil war, they
might be have a more "laissez faire" attitude to their own
safety. If a track is overgrown and not been used for a
while, there's bound to be a reason why, so don't go up
it, it's just not worth the risk.

Improvised Explosive Device (IED)

An IED is essentially an explosive device employed to do
something other than what it was built for. An example
from Afghanistan employed by the Taliban is a 105 mm
artillery shell, concealed in a brick casing, made to look

like a kerb stone by the side of the road to ambush a passing vehicle convoy.

In other forms of attack the insurgents remove the explosive material from the artillery shell and press it into service in another form. They are resourceful, cunning and very good at what they do. The term IED was coined by the British Army in the 1970s after the Provisional Irish Republican Army (PIRA) used bombs made from agricultural fertilizer to make highly effective booby-trap devices or remote-controlled bombs.

An IED typically consists of an explosive charge, a detonator, and an initiation system, which is a mechanism that initiates the electrical charge that sets off the device. IEDs typically also contain shrapnel such as nails or ball bearings (known as shipyard confetti after the metal waste found in the shipyards).

Too large a topic to tackle in detail, I've illustrated a few of the dangerous devices that have been used in the past, it will give you some idea as to the ruthless cunning and ingenuity employed by the insurgents. They are very good at what they do, and are constantly evolving their techniques, if it doesn't work they won't use it. But if it does work it will be widely used and that knowledge will spread, the same successful techniques being used by groups around the world.

Suicide Vehicle Borne IED (SVBIED)

A car, van or motorbike laden with explosives is driven to the target area and detonated. The bomber may well be a committed suicide bomber, and detonate himself and the bomb. However a number of these devices have been found with "chicken switches" which enables an observer some distance away to detonate it himself if he feels that the bomber's resolve is wavering.

Victim Operated IED (VOIED)

A booby trap which could be initiated by using a pressure switch made up of two saw blades mounted on a plank of wood, concealed amongst rubbish on the ground. When stepped on the circuit will be completed and the device functions. These methods have also been used beneath items, so that when they are picked up or disturbed, a spring is released and the circuit is made.

Radio Controlled IED (RCIED)

Detonated from a distance by a radio controlled initiator such as a toy car controller. The hand held controller sends out a signal to tell the toy car to go fwd, turn left etc.. But by tampering with the electronics inside, it can be used to send an electrical current to the device which will cause it to function.

The explosive device can be put in place and when an opportunity target appears, the bomber will strike, and as has been seen they have no regard for civilian casualties.

Command Wire IED (CWIED)

The bomber sits in cover in a good vantage point. He has a battery in one hand and a wire in the other which is leading to a device hidden near a likely passing place. He waits for the target vehicle to drive over it, or for a patrol of soldiers to pass by, he then applies the battery to the wire which detonates the device. Command wires are very hard to spot as they are often well concealed using ditches or rubbish lying around. The further back a Command wire stretches the more power it needs to function, so the longer the wire the bigger the battery. Command wires have been found stretching back 800 metres from the road.

17 ~ Kidnap & Ransom (K&R)

PTSD

Post-Traumatic Stress Disorder or PTSD is sometimes referred to as "Events outside the normal range of human experiences" that the mind found difficult to deal with. This flew in the face of conventional wisdom at the time that it was just fear exposing an inherent weakness in someone's character by winkling in and blowing it out, in the same way that the freeze-thaw actions of ice acts on rock.

At first it was called "Shell shock" but soon renamed "catastrophic stress reaction" after the Great War. Post-Vietnam syndrome followed but admission that this condition existed was swiftly covered up as the scale of the damage to young vets emerged. Any mention vanished without trace in a huge cover up, some say that the difference between schizophrenia and what was to be known as PTSD was that the latter was an admission of human frailty which wasn't palatable to the authorities at the time, this was a very different time to today.

Hostage

The word hostage ironically comes from the Latin *hostis* meaning 'guest', yet being taken hostage is never a pleasant experience. However, it is possible to enhance your chances of survival should you find yourself being held against your will. Lofty Wiseman (the author of the SAS Survival Handbook) suggested that survival is 15% practical and 85% psychological. So in this chapter we'll explore the psychology of hostage taking and how you can use this knowledge to keep yourself alive.

Dangers of Denial

'Be prepared' – is the motto of the Scout movement and sums up one of the key ways in which you can enhance your survival chances and of coping with your captivity. People often do not take account of the dangers in their environment. In everyday life we tend to ignore hazards and so fail to prepare for possible dangerous events. For example, we might not check that our smoke alarms are working as often as we should or we might drive even when the roads are very icy. So why is this? One of the main reasons is that people tend to think '*It will never happen to me.*'

When I lived in California I was surrounded by people who did not have an earthquake kit in their homes. Even though these people were living on the San Andreas Fault, they simply did not believe that they would ever be in a major earthquake.

Denial can be psychologically protective, ignoring the fact that you might be in danger and burying your head in the sand will undoubtedly reduce anxiety. If people in California accepted the very real risk of a major earthquake they would have to think about death and dying, which is psychologically uncomfortable.

When people face dangerous situations you will often find that they distort the warning signs to reassure themselves that they are not in any real danger. However, denial can significantly reduce your survival chances. If you do not fully accept the danger you are in, you may not carry out actions that could save your life, or put yourself in danger when it could have been avoided.

> **"Denial is a strategy... But it's not a very good one"**

Flying to a malaria prone area will increase the risk of contracting this potentially fatal disease. You can respond in one of two ways. First you could deny that you are at risk, and choose to ignore the danger. Or you could go to the doctor and get a supply of anti-malaria pills. Immediately you can see that denial can impact on your survival chances whereas accepting the risk can lead to behaviours that will help you to survive.

So what has this got to do with surviving a hostage taking? Well obviously the best way to survive being taken hostage is to avoid being abducted in the first place. So rather than denying the risks that you may face when you travel to a dangerous area you need to fully understand and accept the risks you are taking so that you can plan accordingly.

Brian Keenan was kidnapped by Islamic Jihad in 1986 and held for four years, he was aware that foreigners living in Beirut were targets for hostage takers. However, he chose to live outside the University campus where he was teaching, without the benefits of security protection. It is possible that Keenan was in denial and although he was aware of the dangers did not believe that he was personally at risk. Therefore, your survival chances are greatly enhanced if you face up to the possible dangers you may face and take the appropriate actions regardless of however psychologically uncomfortable it may be.

The Cost of Preparedness

In addition to denial people also fail to prepare for possible hazards due to cost. Whether that is cost in terms of time, money or effort people are generally reluctant to invest in survival training or equipment. An everyday example of our reluctance to invest can be seen with First Aid training. We should all undertake First Aid training; some people get it free with work and so only have to invest the time and effort whereas others will need to invest money as well.

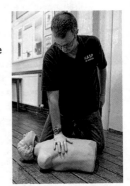

However, not everyone will do a First Aid course and generally in life this will not be a problem – until the day you need it. When you are in a situation where you or someone close to you needs First Aid then that investment becomes worthwhile.

The same is true when people are taken hostage. Those people who have invested the time, effort and money in hostage survival training will be able to draw on that training when needed and so stand a better chance of surviving.

The First Few Moments...

The first few moments of a hostage taking are highly charged and driven by emotion. Even if an abduction has been carefully planned the unpredictability of the victim's response and the danger of getting caught can heighten the adrenaline levels of the hostage taker.

The combination of unpredictable responses and heightened emotion makes this initial phase of a kidnapping one of the most dangerous.

During this period, even if the hostage taker is not under the influence of drugs or suffering from a mental illness, their mental functioning is still likely to be impaired. The hostage taker is therefore likely to be less rational and more liable to react violently. Therefore this is not the time to try and have a rational conversation, as the less you provoke the hostage taker at this time the better.

During the initial abduction it is likely that the hostage will also suffer from impairments in their mental processing. Below are some of the most often reported cognitive failures:-

• **Freezing or Cognitive Paralysis** – when people face serious threats it is normally assumed that we will make one of two responses, fight or flight.' However,

Dr John Leach of the University of Oslo suggests there is a third behavioral response which he has termed Cognitive Paralysis. Cognitive Paralysis refers to when '*anxiety in a life threatening situation becomes so overwhelming that it induces a form of paralysis.*' This type of freezing has been reported in people being taken hostage. For example, the CBS journalist, Jere Van Dyk, when was kidnapped by the Taliban noted that he initially froze when faced armed kidnappers.

- **Denial behaviours** – People can try to reassure themselves during the initial stages of a kidnapping that everything is ok. For example, Missionaries Martin and Gracia Burnham, who were kidnapped and held for a year by terrorists in the Philippines tried to explain the gunshots they heard in their beach resort as being the result of a drunken guard. Although denial can be dangerous as it can stop people from facing up to the full gravity of the situation, it can also act as a defence mechanism allowing people to cope when they feel that they may be overwhelmed by a situation.

- **Weapon focus** – hostages can generally give very good descriptions of the hostage taker's weapons but can be remarkably poor at describing the actual hostage taker. Victims of violent crimes commonly report perceptual narrowing where their focus becomes fixated upon the weapon the assailant is carrying. This means that hostages are generally very poor at recalling simple details such as the height or hair colour of the hostage taker.

- **Problems with decision-making** – hostages may find it harder to think clearly and make rational decisions. Many reasons may cause this failure in mental processing (or as Dr John Leach terms it Cognitive Dysexecutive Syndrome). Thinking and decision making may be impaired due to increases in anxiety (and the associated changes in neurochemistry). Or failures could be due to the brain not having enough processing power to make the decisions needed in a very novel situation within a limited time frame.

You should be aware that during the trauma period of the abduction, it may not be possible to think clearly and devise rationale actions. Normal mental functioning will return for most hostages but with training it is possible to increase your ability to think rationally during periods of acute stress.

The Importance of Training

Making rational decisions and thinking clearly during those first few moments of a kidnapping could mean the difference between survival and death. If you are able to take in and respond to the situation you may stand a better chance of staying alive or even escaping during those initial chaotic moments.

However, people are generally very poor at carrying out useful actions under pressure but this can be improved with training. Think about the first time you tried to drive a car. Most people during their first driving lesson find it difficult to cope with the number of decisions and actions which need to be completed.

Once you have had a few lessons and some of those actions have become automatic you are able to drive competently, responding to the new situations and act accordingly. Training can also help you to respond appropriately during a hostage taking. If you have practised your responses and think through the possible actions you might take in certain situations in advance then you are much more likely to be able to generate those useful responses at the critical moment.

Therefore, quality training perhaps including a simulated hostage taking can be helpful as in the event that you are caught up in a real hostage situation your responses will be pre-planned and therefore you are more likely to be able to carry them out.

Time to Negotiate

When a hostage is taken for financial or political gains it can end in one of two ways, either with the use of force or by negotiation. Over the last thirty years there has been a move away from the use of force (which often ended with loss of life) towards negotiations. Negotiations are likely to continue as long as the hostage(s) are deemed not to be in immediate danger.

However as Ben Lopez in his book 'The Negotiator' points out, taking your time with negotiations can be critical for a successful resolution.

- Hostage taking is a psychologically stressful time for the hostage taker as well as the hostage. During the initial snatch emotions will be running high on both sides. The adrenaline will be pumping and aggressive levels are likely to be high whereas the ability to think rationally is likely to have disappeared. Therefore slowing down the negotiations allows arousal levels to reduce. The perpetrator, with time, is likely to become less emotional and anxious and will be more likely to engage in rational discussions.

- Slowing down negotiations gives more time for an intelligence picture to be drawn up. Other agencies will be trying to gather information on possible locations of hostages, the background of the hostage takers and other information which could help if an armed resolution to the crisis is needed.

- Taking a long time with negotiations can also act as a deterrent. Lopez points out that on situations where the motive is financial if a hostage taker is paid too soon they may well strike again as they have made good money in a short period of time. If the negotiations are more drawn out then the cost of keeping the hostage and the time required to gain the ransom may well put a hostage taker off from acting again.

- Time allows a relationship to build between the perpetrators and negotiator. The negotiator is likely to use a system such as the FBI's 'Behavioural Influence Stairway Model' to build a relationship. Using techniques such as these the negotiator will try to persuade the hostage taker to release the hostage and so ensure a peaceful conclusion to the kidnapping. However, the techniques take time as trust needs to be built.

- Time also allows a relationship to build between the hostage taker and the hostage. If the hostage taker starts to see the hostage as a person and not simply a means to an end then this can help to keep the hostage alive and hopefully result in a successful outcome.

Staying Alive

After the initial shock of capture comes the adaption phase where people start to accept the reality and adjust to their new situation. Humans are very adaptable and are able to cope with the demanding situations. For example, people can live in all sorts of environments from Polar Research Stations to the depths of the jungle. However, for adaptation to occur it is important that basic psychological and physical needs are met. Once a person's basic needs are met people are then able to function normally.

1. **Physical needs** – the body is very susceptible to restrictions in food and water. Both are critical for survival. In a hostage situation it is important that if you are offered food or water that you take it. This might in some circumstances involve eating food which does not appear that appealing but you need to overcome your revulsion. Without fuel your brain and body will not function as affectively as they need to.

2. **Try and get as much sleep and rest as possible.** Without sleep mental processing will start to suffer and clear thinking be difficult if not impossible.

3. **Dependence on legal drugs** such as nicotine (cigarettes) and caffeine (from tea, coffee or cola) can also be difficult to deal with. If either of these substances are suddenly removed (as any smoker who has attempted to give up will tell you) then thinking clearly can be difficult. People in high risk areas may wish to think about reducing their dependence on these substances.

4. **Keep physically fit if possible** and take any opportunity for exercise. Exercise has two main benefits. First it can help to relieve the boredom of the situation and so can help relieve symptoms of anxiety and depression by giving you a task to focus on. Second, keeping fit can mean that you are physically able to cope if negotiations break down and the hostage taking is ended by force.

5. **Overcoming boredom** can be a major problem during extended hostage situations. Terry Waite, who was held by Islamic Jihad for a number of years, noted that his day consisted of *'Bread and lebne for breakfast, one quick visit to the bathroom, and the twenty-three hours and fifty minutes lying in the corner with nothing but my thoughts.'* Both Keenan and Waite in their autobiographies highlight the importance of creating a schedule for tasks and setting goal to allow a sense of achievement. Waite asked for a radio or reading material to help pass the time. Whereas Keenen reported that he made a chess and scrabble set in order to keep his mind active and his mental health in check.

6. **Some hostages have reported particular problems** associated with being held in isolation. Keenan, for example, experienced both visual and auditory hallucinations when he was held on his own in a bare cell. His reported auditory hallucinations *'like a tribal chant; great orchestras of violins and flutes filling the air like bird flight....I kept telling myself 'There is no music Brian, it's all in your head.'* Hallucinations

are common when we are in a sensory deprived environment and it is important to note that it is not evidence that you are losing your mind. Hallucinations can occur in mentally healthy individuals after as little as 15 minutes of being confirmed to a room devoid of stimuli. It is thought that the hallucinations occur as the brain tries to make sense of the reduction in stimuli and misattributes internal thoughts and feelings as occurring outside in the environment.

7. **Humans are social creatures** and a shared experience can reduce the anxiety of the situation. More hostages held in isolation report mental health problems than those held in a group. Keenan on being moved to a shared cell with John McCarthy (the journalist who had been kidnapped while trying to make a documentary about Keenan) talked about the *'warmth, intimacy and companionship which came flooding to us both.'*

Improving your Resilience

Some people appear to be able to adapt to new environments with ease and are more resilient when placed in hostile situations. Other people appear more susceptible to physical and mental harm as a result of being taken hostage. What makes some people better able to cope with new and challenging situations is an interesting question and one that psychologists are only now starting to answer.

Resilience in everyday life has been found to be linked to our levels of optimism. One psychologist, Martin Seligman, suggests that how optimistic you are about your circumstances influences how well you are able to cope with anything from unemployment through to illness. Walter Busuttil, the Medical Director and Consultant psychiatrist for Combat Stress, suggests that optimism is also important for hostages.

Hostages who have a conviction that they will survive appear to have better outcomes. One of the possible reasons for this is that if you think you are going to survive you are more likely to engage in behaviours that will increase survival chances.

Furthermore the opposite is also true, when people lose hope such as the World War II prisoners of war who suffered from apathy syndrome (a lack of motivation to do anything) then their drive to survive disappeared.

So how do we stay optimistic when times are tough? One method some people adopt is to draw on religious beliefs. When writing  about their hostage experiences both Terry Waite and Gracia Burnham often comment on how their faith was important in helping them to keep going when their circumstances became difficult.

For example, Gracia Burnham notes that during an exchange of gunfire she prayed to God asking him to *"Keep us safe and keep me sane."* By believing that things will be ok and that rescue is just around the corner you are more likely to stay calm and act in a positive way. Just by being optimistic about your situation you are more likely to carry out actions that make survival more likely.

Another driving force which appears to give hostages the motivation to survive is strong attachments to family or friends. People who have been held against their will, such as survivors of concentration camps, often report that the need to see their partner or a child again gives them a very strong motivation to survive.

Focusing on goals, such as to see a loved one again, can help to maintain resilience during difficult times.

Your Relationship with the Hostage Taker

The way in which you interact with a hostage taker can be critical to your survival. Hostage takers may try to dehumanise hostages by covering their faces or refusing to address them by their names. It is much easier to be violent towards a nameless unidentified person than to someone that is actually a person with thoughts and feelings.

Therefore, if possible, you need to get the hostage takers to identify with you, to start to see you as a person. For example, Martin and Gracia Burnham shared their Christian faith with their Muslim captors, highlighting similarities between Christianity and Islam. Gracia Burnham also used information about her children to generate common ground between her captors and herself.

One of the most commonly described relationship between a hostage and a hostage taker is development of Stockholm syndrome. This type of relationship was first observed during a robbery of a bank in Stockholm, Sweden in 1973. During the robbery four bank employees were held by two robbers in a bank vault. The hostages appeared to become emotionally attached to their captors and afterwards the hostages even defended their hostage takers actions.

Another possible incidence of Stockholm syndrome is the case of Patty Hearst, the daughter of William Hearst, a newspaper tycoon, who was kidnapped by the Symbionese Liberation Army in 1974. After being held for two months she appeared to have started to believe the propaganda and even took an active part in an armed bank robbery. Although it is thought that the development of Stockholm syndrome is quite rare it can be useful in keeping the hostage alive.

The hostage taker is less likely to kill or injure a person who they feel is on their side. However, Stockholm syndrome can also have a dangerous side. Hostages who develop Stockholm syndrome may not help if a hostage taking is ended by force and in some situations may even resist a rescue attempt.

Another relationship seen during hostage situations is London syndrome. London syndrome was coined after the 1980 siege in the Iranian embassy in London. On the sixth day one of the hostages was shot and his body thrown on to the street. Reports from other hostages within the embassy suggest that the victim, Abbas Lavasani, had developed a very antagonistic relationship with his captors, continually challenging them both verbally and physically.

A final relationship which has been observed is Lima syndrome. Lima syndrome was first observed during the Japanese embassy hostage crisis of 1996 which lasted over five months. During the siege the hostage takers actually began to sympathise with the hostages. This sympathy led to many of the hostages being released.

Stockholm, London and Lima syndromes are likely to be the extremes of the types of relationships which may start to form during a hostage situation. Generally, in order to survive, the best policy is not to stand out from the crowd if you are taken hostage with a group of people.

Being the 'grey man' and fading into the background can be the best policy avoiding direct eye contact if possible. Being confrontational can put the hostage takers on edge and this can result in you being singled out. On the other hand if conditions deteriorate then try and humanise yourself in the eyes of your captor as this may help you to avoid more violent treatment.

Thoughts of Home?

When a person is taken hostage the consequences are not just felt by the victim. The hostage is likely to have family (parents, a partner and/or children) as well as close friends who can also be deeply affected by the situation. Family and friends can be seen as secondary victims of the hostage taking and will need both practical and emotional help. If a person knows that they are at high risk of being kidnapped then it is worth having a discussion before they go about what to do if the worst happens.

Some families may not wish to face up to the risks that a loved one may be taking and may seek to deny that the situation might occur. Denial can mean that both sides are unwilling to discuss practical issues such as life insurance or writing a will.

However, if you have planned for the worst at least you know that your loved ones are better prepared for the tough times ahead. Below are some key points which should be discussed.

- Make sure that you have a 'what if' plan written with key names and addresses of people to contact, such as employer's details or the phone number of the British Embassy.
- Make sure that partners/family know about support groups which could help if the worst was to happen. For example, Hostage UK is a charity that can help families cope during and after a kidnapping.
- Make sure that if a kidnapping does occur family have the financial means to cope. Hostage families can find that employers stop paying wages and so may not have enough money to survive on.

- If the hostage taking is financially motivated a large ransom may have to be raised. Families should discuss whether hostage insurance should be considered.
- Write a will. Everyone over the age of 18 should write a will and this is especially true for people working in high risk areas. If you find yourself in potentially life-threatening situations it can be comforting to know that if the worst should happen your loved ones are provided for.

Shock of Rescue

A hostage situation can end in a number of ways but the two most common are law-enforcement agencies rescuing the hostages by force, or the hostages being released as a result of the negotiations. Either way, the end phase of a hostage taking can be as dangerous as the initial abduction, with high levels of emotion impairing the mental functioning of hostage, the hostage taker and in some cases the rescue team.

If a hostage siege is to be ended by force, a hostage should try to identify themselves as a hostage as you do not want to be mistaken for a hostage taker at this point. Further, it is critical that you remain aware of the environment, move away from points of entry such as windows and doors, and try to shield yourself from flying glass and other hazards.

One key observation is that after someone has been rescued they can suffer from a cognitive collapse. That is to say that immediately after rescue victims can become dazed, withdrawn, and passive.

This loss of the 'drive to survive' can be fatal if the victims are not in a place of safety. Try to be self-aware of your own functioning and do not relax until you are completely sure that you are in a safe place.

Return and Adaptation

Many people think that once a hostage has been released that is the end of the story. The media lose interest after the hostage has been reunited with their family and the victim is expected to slot back into everyday life. And for some former hostages this is the case.

The trauma of the event is placed in the past and they are able to move forward with their lives with few ill effects. For others the return home is not as straightforward and their experiences may make the adjustment back into their old lives difficult. In the past psychologists and other health care professionals have been very quick to jump in with interventions designed to help people cope with the trauma they have experienced.

However, recently research has suggested that this approach actually causes more harm and that a period of 'watchful waiting' is more appropriate.

Watchful waiting basically means that former hostages will be assessed over a period of 4-6 weeks from a distance to see if they are exhibiting any severe negative responses to their experience. Only if the former hostage shows signs of Post-Traumatic Stress Disorder, depression, anxiety, substance abuse or suicidal thoughts will interventions be considered appropriate.

Check List of PTSD Symptoms

- **Re-experiencing** – reliving the kidnapping can take the form of images, nightmares or flashbacks.
- **Avoidance** – Avoiding situations, places or actions that can remind the person of the hostage taking.
- **Hyper arousal** – High levels of anxiety which mean that people consistently feel 'on edge' and that they are unable to relax.
- **Emotional numbing** – After a kidnapping some people may try to block out all feelings and can become withdrawn.
- **Mood changes** – after being taken hostage some people can become depressed or anxious and this can also lead to a number of physical symptoms such as shaking, headaches or dizziness.
- **Substance misuse** – some people try to control or block out their feelings by turning to drink or drugs.

Some former hostages may suffer from Survivor guilt - they may feel guilty that they survived when others did not or that they were unable to help other hostages. Gracia Burnham, for example, suffered from Survivor guilt after her husband Martin during a rescue attempt.

She questioned her actions asking '*What if I'd spoken to him and tried to wake him up? What if I'd rolled him over so the bleeding wouldn't have filled up his lungs so fast? Would he still be alive?*' This type of guilt can be very damaging for the survivor and can stop them from readapting and moving forward with their life.

Professional counselling can be needed to help the victim to come to terms with the actions that they took in the heat of the moment and to help free them from the sense of blame that they carry.

It should also be remembered that it is not only the hostage who has gone through a traumatic experience. For the family and friends of the victim the thought of losing a loved one can also be very traumatic. Once a hostage returns home the victim's friends and family should also be assessed for signs of secondary traumatisation as they may also suffer from the problems listed in the PTSD checklist.

Post Traumatic Growth

Nietzsche suggests that 'What doesn't kill you makes you stronger' and some former hostages have suggested that the trauma they experienced did have some positive effects on their lives. These positive effects are referred to in the literature as post traumatic growth and highlight how experiencing trauma does not always cause negative reactions. People who experience post traumatic growth say that their experiences have increased their levels of confidence and their self-belief. They also report that their relationships with family and friends have been strengthened and they have a new determination to 'seize the day'

References

Burnham, G. with Merrill, D. (2003). *In the presence of my enemies.* Illinois: Tyndale House Publishers. (Page 89 for quote regarding optimism, and page 272 for the quote regarding survivor guilt)

Busuttil, W. (2008). Prolonged incarceration: Effects on hostages of Terrorism. *Journal of the Royal Army Medical Corps.* *154(2): 128-135* assessed from *http://www.ramcjournal.com/2008/jun08/busutill.pdf*

Firman, R. & Pearson, W. (2010). *Go! Go! Go! The definitive inside story of the Iranian Embassy Siege.* London: The Orion Publishing House Ltd.

Keenan, B. (1992). *An Evil Cradling.* London: Hutchinson. (Page 78 for quote)

Leach, J. (1994). *Survival Psychology.* Basingstoke, Hants: Palgrave Macmillan

Lopez, B. (2011). *The Negotiator. My life at the heart of the Hostage Trade.* St Ives: Sphere.

Seligman, M. (1998). *Learned Optimism.* New York: Pocket Books

Van Dyk, J. (2010). *Captive: My time as a prisoner of the Taliban.* New York: Time Books. (Quote from page 53)

Waite, T. (1993). *Taken on Trust.* London: Hodder and Stoughton. (Page 81 for the quote).

18 ~ Who, What and Where...

Medical Kit

Hostile environment training preparation is a rough 50/50 split between security and medical/first aid topics. At HASP Training our medical director is Stuart Wilson, who also operates Athena Medical Services that supplies all our medical kits. I asked him to write a few words of wisdom about how to assemble a medical kit tailored for your trip.

Stuart - Medical kits come is all shapes and sizes. Some are standard workplace first aid kits that contain a legally required list of items. They are designed to be used by a member of staff who has limited first aid training; the kits increase in size to cover larger numbers of employees.

They are basic and cover most minor injuries but are designed to be used only when the local Emergency services are already on their way to the incident. Whoever is the 'nominated' first aider has to then document the injury and replace the items that have been used.

There is no 'trauma' equipment included, so there are no tourniquets, airways or other such lifesaving items. This is because these kits are NOT designed for use in severe trauma and the nominated first aider has not been trained to deal with such incidents.

At the opposite end of the scale is a full paramedic trauma bag that has advanced trauma life support equipment, analgesia, oxygen and possibly a defibrillator as well. All of this will be heavy, bulky and will take up a lot of space.

If you are traveling by air, all compressed gas (oxygen) will be classed as Dangerous Air Cargo (DAC) and there are separate regulations for each airline about carrying such items. Do not arrive at a point of departure without prior permission or your equipment WILL be confiscated. If you are travelling to remote or hostile locations find out beforehand if there are any items that you cannot take.

When you are putting together your own medical kit you have to consider several factors first.

1. Space: how much space do you have?

2. Will the kit be in a pocket or pouch that is integral to an existing Bergan or rucksack?

3. Do you want to use an existing pouch that has been specifically designed or utilise a standard pouch?

4. Will you require a brightly coloured pack that is obvious a medical pack or a dark, tactical colour?

5. How far will you have to carry it? Or will it be in a vehicle?

6. Will this be the only medical kit or will each team member have an Individual pack of their own?

7. Can you use everything that you are carrying?

Understand your task, what is the job? Evaluate the risks, research what kind of injuries will you have to deal with? What type of environment is it? Is it hot or cold? And how will that impact on those you are providing cover for? What are the local insects and reptiles?

One thing you must never do is OVER PACK! You cannot carry something for every single scenario or you will be carrying a massive pack full of very heavy equipment that you may never use.

The kit sizes that you can look at are:
- Individual
- Small Team (2 – 4 people)
- Medium (4 – 8)
- Large (8 – 20)
- Extra Large (20 +)

You can purchase pre-packed kits, but you may find yourself removing items that you are unlikely to use and buying additional pieces. There are some suppliers that will build a 'custom' kit for you but these will be more expensive.

Individual

These kits contain items that are for the individual to use on themselves in a trauma situation. This will normally be 1/2 tourniquets, 1 pressure dressing and a very small amount of primary care (plasters and very mild pain relief i.e. para-cetamol) and any medication that is required for pre-existing conditions.

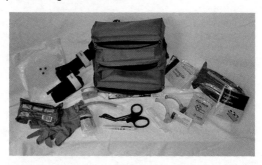

Small Team

This is for a small number of people over a short period of time without resupply. You start with the individual kit and build on it. You may want 1 or 2 extra tourniquets, more dressings and certainly more airways. Included in this you may pack scissors, tape, a tri-bandage, a chest seal and possibly a burns dressing. This will be suitable for 1 – 2 major casualties.

Medium

This is a larger kit to be used for a longer period of time or a larger number of serious trauma casualties. You will now want to include splintage, fluid replacement, haemostatic bandages and diagnostic items such as a fingertip pulse oximeter, Blood sugar monitor and a stethoscope. You can add more primary care items to this kit.

Large

In a large kit you will be carrying at least 4 tourniquets and a larger amount of pressure dressings, haemostatic bandages and diagnostic items. If you are going to be in a remote location you will have to increase the amount of primary care that you are carrying.

Extra Large

The extra-large kit enables you to cover a larger number of people and to be self-sufficient for a longer period of time. This is the type of kit that you would take to a base camp or permanent location and support with smaller/ medium kits for tasking out and about.
Athena Medical Services

Based in London and online www.athenamedicalservices.co.uk are our first port of call for all our medical kits and training.

Grab Bags

Whenever I travel anywhere I carry a little bag with me, the contents of which will vary from location to location and depend on what I am doing.

When I went to Florida with my wife and 1 year old daughter last year on holiday, my little bag contained my iPad, book, travel adaptor to charge phone, sun glasses, sun cream etc...

We knew we were never very far away from food, medical services and so we could chill out and enjoy the holiday (well as much as a toddler will allow you to).

Although because Congress couldn't decide on the budget the airport staff were on a go slow and it took us over 3 hours to get through the gate.

We didn't have our daughter's buggy (which was in the hold) so we held her in our arms which you can imagine with a 1 year old was a bit of a nightmare. All I can say is thank goodness for free kids games on the iPad or we would have been in trouble

When I went to Kabul to teach cartooning for 10 days to a group of Illustrators, my bag contained 20 passport photos for all the various permits I thought I might have to get at the airport, a phrase book, a small med kit, travel plug (I knew little about my accommodation) etc...

I have a box in the garage marked "Grab Bag" which contains the following stuff which I occasionally add to when I come across something new. I have divided it into 5 different sections: **Staying Occupied – There - Well – Fed – Safe.**

We stock a ready to go HASP Grab Bag with most of the contents below, so keep an eye on our website *www.hasptraining.co.uk* for more info.

Hasp Grab Bag Contents

Staying Occupied

IPod / Magazine / Notebook and some pencils / Phrasebook / Universal Power adaptor / Couple of biros / Power monkey / Playing cards / Travel pillow.

I don't particularly like being bored or sitting around doing nothing, but neither do I mind sitting on a bench waiting for a delayed plane for 4-5 hours. As long as I have got a few things to do. Which is why I always tuck a few things in my bag to keep me busy, I love reading the Economist (but rarely get the chance to read it each week from cover to cover) so I always have this week's copy if I am out and about.

Staying There

Compass / Map / Gaffer tape / Waterproof pouch for mobile.

Staying Well

Antibacterial wipes / Sun cream / Tooth brush / Small med kit including a few wet wipes / Imodium / Hand wash / Tiger balm / Mosquito repellent / Mosquito head net / Travel plug / Bin bags / Kleenex tissues / Cap / Sun glasses / Multivitamin tablets / your own set of travel cutlery.

If you get stuck in an area with very scant medical services, a filthy dirty hotel or guest house and you've got nothing to protect you from infection, then it won't be long before you succumb. But pack a few things on the list to clean your hands and fingers regularly then you should keep a lid on it.

Staying Fed

Plastic Cup / Spoon / Can of coke or water / Snacks (this could be loosely based around a camping ration pack, chocolate bar few tea bags etc... the sort of thing that would be a headache to procure down the route but would be a little life saver in the right circumstances).

Staying Safe

Door wedge and rape alarm / Co2 and smoke alarm / Money belt or shoulder belt / Head torch with spare batteries / Robber's wallet / Para cord / Whistle / Gerber multi tool / small padlock.

You can use the gaffer tape to attach the rape alarm to the door of your hotel if you're concerned about people breaking in. Smoke alarms and Co2 alarms are a great idea in many countries because H&S is a concept that hasn't readily caught on.

Head torches are a fantastic invention, if the hotel you're staying in is prone to random blackouts don't be without it in your pocket. A robber's wallet with a few bank notes kept in the other pocket might be enough to satisfy a mugger.

HASP Grab Bags

I mentioned earlier that we stock HASP Grab Bags, keep an eye on the website or give us a call, getting one from us will save you time and £££.

It'll probably take you an entire weekend of traipsing around the shops/web to procure it all and will cost a small fortune.

A friend of mine runs an outdoor shop and gets all the kit at trade. We can supply it in its own HASP bag or you can just purchase the contents and put it in your own favourite bag. See the website for more details
www.hasptraining.co.uk

Northcott Global Solutions

Northcott Global Solutions Ltd
Global Emergency Response
Tel: +44 207 183 8 9 10
www.northcottglobalsolutions.com

NGS is the new generation of *"Evacuation and Contingency Response"* companies whose services reflect modern travel patterns with more firms venturing into the developing world in search of business opportunities.

Reactive by nature, but vigorously Proactive in its attitude to preparation ensures that their clients deploy with the correct level of support in place already. And you don't need to be a large multinational either, NGS has a range of solutions to suit budgets and itineraries, from issuing individuals with a "Pearl" Pocket Buddy to a comprehensive trip tracking set up for a large team.

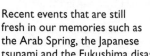

Recent events that are still fresh in our memories such as the Arab Spring, the Japanese tsunami and the Fukushima disaster that followed (not to mention the Syrian civil war) exposed organizations who claimed to offer this service. NGS stepped in when other suppliers who offered this capability had seriously let down their clients.

Examples:

Yemen - NGS took 3 hours to get a BBC Hard Talk team out of Yemen after they were directly threatened by a local Al Qaeda team in country. That's *180* minutes from making the call to wheels up on the plane getting them out.

Japan - NGS took 2 hours to supply fuel to an 8 man ITN crew stranded by the Japanese Tsunami, getting them back on the road.

Afghanistan – NGS arranged a dental appointment 600 yards away for an Insurance underwriter in Kabul at a cost of $400 when they had previously had to fly their staff to Dubai, which would have been a little bit more costly.

Libya – The Ops team were able to get 11 oil workers out of Libya on a ferry almost immediately after the unrest there, and because they already had a relationship with NGS it didn't cost them a bean.

Mali – When a coup took place in Mali, a large US Logistics company phoned their emergency provider and were told that nothing could be done. Local airspace was closed, but within 3 hours the NGS team had them over the border into Burkina Faso and in the air.

These are just a few examples of the achievements of Ted, Marcus and Richards' set up in the heart of the

City of London in the shadow of the Gherkin. The NGS' state-of-the-art 24/7 Operations Room is manned by experienced, calm, efficient ex-Senior members of the British Armed Forces who are used to operating under pressure.

The Ops team provide a "Point of Incident" Response by using its network of pre-approved Service Providers. This combination of capability and local knowledge allows NGS to "Press GO" on a **Swift - Efficient - Secure** response when the phone rings.

NGS has a growing global network of over 5,000 Service Providers from interpreters and private ambulances, to helicopters and 4x4 vehicles. They undertake detailed Due Diligence on all their service providers ensuring they have the necessary insurances and accreditation.

So you know you'll get the same efficient friendly service if are picked up from your hotel in Bamako for a quick race to the airport or visit the office in London to discuss your trip with the guys.

Itinerary Tracking, Real Time
Tracking, Safety Check Calls and
Mass Notification-warning &
informing systems are a few of
the NGS Services that support &
enhance our Emergency Assistance
model.

NGS' clients include some of the
largest Mining, Oil & Gas, Media and
Banking corporations, highlighting the
gap that the NGS Point of Incident
Evacuation and Crisis Management
Model has filled.

For NGS Evacuation is the last
resort. Why desert your location when perhaps
hibernating in place or re-locating locally might be the
better option. Having the ability to track your employyes
has allowed a revolution in Kidnap response resolving
situations in hours.

Terrorism Research & Analysis Consortium

www.tracterrorism.org
Veryan Khan, Editorial Director
vkhan@tracterrorism.org

TRAC Terrorism – it's not difficult to figure out what Veryan and her team do and how useful it could be to you when you are doing your pre-trip research. She has assembled a worldwide authoritative network of experts and editors, commissioning reports on terrorist groups, their ideologies, tactics and targets.

Veryan's team live, work and report from some of the world's most notorious hotspots - including Russia, Poland, Egypt, Lebanon, Israel, India, Pakistan, Singapore, Bangladesh, Malaysia, Philippines, Bulgaria, Croatia, Azerbaijan, Afghanistan and Serbia.

This gives researchers a 360° view of "on the ground" activity of political violence and terrorism. Research in 10 minutes what took TRAC 10 years to develop.

TRAC offers insight into an array of situations: from researching groups and affiliations, tactics and weapons, to fast-breaking news about who was where.

Strong emphasis is maintained on helping researchers

locate the most up to date information with one of the largest databases of current and historical groups in the world – updated daily. 4,200+ terrorist groups, their leaders, locations and affiliations with other groups.

The Chatter Control Centre monitors web feeds and news from around the world and posts stories as they occur. The team archives and indexes web material related to terrorism and political violence. It then links it to TRAC's database, making it a one-stop portal for anyone researching political violence.

Features

Original in-depth analysis of important terrorism issues from: Gender and Terrorism to Quranic Understandings of Violent Jihad to Vulnerable Cities and Urban Terrorism.

- Profiles of 4,200+ groups that have been known to aid and abet political violence or terrorist organizations. Each profile includes (when known) the group's tactics, targets, ideology, associated groups, leaders, theatre of operation
- Resources: think tanks, government agencies, universities, community colleges, and police academies offering courses in terrorism.
- Profiles of vulnerable regions and cities most likely to attract terrorist incidents.
- Access to political violence experts worldwide.
- Continuous collection of information from media and primary resources collectively, painting a picture of the real situation on the ground.
- Publishing opportunities - TRAC provides a publishing centre for research of any length produced by its members.
- Chatter Control - TRAC continuously monitors the

important news and analyses sources and posts feeds to the site as they happen.

- Contributors reporters and Consortium members can post stories and have them immediately disbursed throughout the network.

Subscriptions

TRAC offers subscription services to institutions. The license rate is prorated by the size, number of facilities and number of patrons/students/faculty of the institution, and ranges from $1,000 to $10,000/year.

Subscribing institutions have unlimited use of the website and may reproduce or distribute TRAC data for use within their institution.

Dignity Hostage Survival Consultancy

www.dignity-hsc.com
Telephone: +44 (0) 7789 278329

DHSC we believe it is vital for staff working in, or visiting high risk countries to be properly equipped and prepared to deal with the risk of becoming a victim of a kidnapping. As well as the impact on the individual concerned and their families, friends and colleagues, the reputation and business of your company may be put at risk (internally and externally) if one of your executives, employees, or their family, is taken hostage or kidnapped by criminals or terrorists.

Based on detailed hostage debriefings, input from survival psychologists and security expertise, we offer our clients (i.e. potential targets) proven methods and strategies for maintaining their physical and psychological well-being in a very stressful situation to improve their resilience during captivity and after release.

We provide an in depth pre-travel security briefing, specific to your organization, for staff identified as potentially at risk, in all aspects of Hostage Survival/ Awareness, which covers the following:

- Motives of a Hostage Taker
- Situation Assessment
- Stages of Abduction
- Rapport Building Strategies
- Captivity pressures
- Coping Strategies
- End of Captivity

We also offer a guest speaker who has actually survived a hostage/kidnap experience and can reinforce and emphasize the importance of this briefing, can also be provided.

Reintegration: after victims are released, they are likely to require support in recovering from their ordeal and reintegrating successfully back into society. We offer a range of expert advice including in the fields of psychology, life coaching, and former hostage mentors, who can provide advice during and after a hostage ordeal.

DHSC also has links with insurers who provide K&R insurance directly linked to a crisis/incident management team and experienced hostage negotiators. Our Hostage Awareness package forms part of their K&R prevention offer to clients.

As part of our reintegration programme, we offer training for a company's HR staff to deal with these situations, to become 'defusers', to minimize the risk damaging the relationships between the company the individual, and their families. We can provide crisis media support, for the company and the family, in the event of a kidnapping/hostage taking.

Dr Sarita Robinson

The Best Survival Training has to be Reality-Based

Dr Sarita Robinson
Chartered Psychologist and BPS member
Fellow of the Institute of Civil Protection and
Emergency Management.

Sarita has actively researched psychological responses to threat for over 15 years. Sarita's PhD under the supervision of Dr John Leach at Lancaster University explored the neurochemical and psychological changes in people undergoing Helicopter Underwater Escape and FireFighter training at the Nautical College in Fleetwood.

She has since gone on to work with the Defence Science and Technology Laboratory, Health Protection Agency, and Norwegian Defence Intelligence and Security School.

A vital ingredient in any survival situation is the mental attitude of those involved.

Having survival skills is important; having the will to survive is essential. Our course on Survival Psychology will train you to:

• Prepare yourself psychologically before travelling to high risk environments such as war zones
• Handle high pressure situations
• Survive as a potential hostage
• Provide support and reassurance for your family and friends at home
• Recover and reintegrate

Delivered by Dr Sarita Robinson, this flexible one-day training course is available 7 days a week.

Get in touch to request a date and find out more.

CiC: Employee Wellbeing, Resilience and Trauma Support

Kate Nowlan, Chief Executive, CiC Employee Assistance

When you're working overseas, you might find yourself in an unfamiliar environment and one that is likely to throw up some challenging or dangerous situations and scenarios. Despite your earnest preparations when you're working in this type of environment there may be circumstances that put you under extraordinary pressure.

When this type of trauma happens, you're going to need to be resilient. And the best way to be resilient is to invest as much time as you have available to prepare for your assignment and ensure you have a strong insight into how your mind and body will react to a traumatic situation.

CiC helps its clients prepare for and cope with extraordinary pressures that can be involved in working overseas. After all, stress and trauma can strike employees and organisations in many different ways; whilst critical incidents such as the death of a colleague or violent attacks will have a devastating impact, it's also true that subtler, cumulative stressors such as organizational change, tight budgets and poor internal communications will also have a deeply corrosive effect on employee wellbeing.

So to ensure that employees are supported in their assignments overseas, **CiC Global Stress and Trauma Support services** combines clinical expertise, commercial acumen and frontline experience of stress and trauma management to help keep employees safe and support them whether they need a rapid response or ongoing support at every stage of their overseas posting:

- **Before assignment...** you'll need to know the emotional and physical risks ahead, make reliable arrangements to stay in touch, identify and adopt some reliable self-care strategies, and understand how you'll stay in touch with your manager and key contacts at home.

- **During assignment...** you'll want to keep in regular contact with work, family and friends and keep up-to-date about what's happening at home.

- **After assignment...** you should expect to de-brief about your experiences and offer feedback to your employees. You should also receive access to practical support and assistance from trained counsellors and therapists, should you require longer term support.

Services such as **CiC's International Adviceline** mean that confidential telephone assistance is available to employees and managers 24 hours a day, seven days a week. This type of service provides comprehensive emotional and practical support in just about any language.

There may also be times on assignment when you need help on the ground. In response to terrorist attacks, armed bank raids, rail and plane crashes, industrial accidents and workplace deaths and suicides, **CiC's Critical Incident Support** team are on hand to offer on-site support and counselling. This, combined with longer-term psychological support, enables individuals to be more resilient to crisis and trauma situations.

Learning and development is also a key part of creating a resilient workforce and CiC's interactive seminars and workshops are designed for managers, giving them the tools and techniques to take responsibility for their own stress as well as promoting the emotional wellbeing of their staff. Some of the most popular issues that managers sign up for include:

- Understanding human reactions to a crisis
- Identifying common signs of stress
- Understanding organisational and group responses to an emergency
- Recognising the impact of cumulative stress
- Devising positive wellbeing strategies to alleviate symptoms and enhance resilience
- Building culturally relevant interventions for international programmes

Understanding different types of stress

When it comes to identifying the common signs of stress, there are some clear indications that you or your colleagues may need to implement some self-care strategies or seek professional support and assistance from, for example, an Employee Assistance Programme such as Confidential Care from CiC. This is an independent, free and completely confidential service that offers assistance for whatever issue or problem you're facing.

Cumulative stress – warning signs that stress is creeping up on you

- Headaches, back pain, insomnia
- Depression, anxiety, mood swings, apathy, irritability
- Forgetfulness, poor concentration, boredom, paranoia, poor teamwork
- Loneliness, withdrawal, intolerance, relationship problems
- Heavy drinking, earing problems, overwork
- Sense of emptiness

Acute stress – indications that you're reaching burnout

- Chronic sleeping disorders and exhaustion
- Deterioration of mental capacities
- Memory loss
- Loss of self-esteem, focus on failure
- Profound disillusionment, rejection of values
- Refusal to take holiday
- Taking unnecessary risks
- Panic or anxiety attacks
- Severe depression and addiction

Our experience has taught us that one of the best ways of dealing with trauma and stress-related problems, particularly when you're working overseas, is through good social support from colleagues, managers, friends and family, combined with effective and consistent self-care. This can involve simple yet highly effective techniques, including accepting that your responses are